Basic Understanding
of
Mutual Funds

Book 7

For Teens
and Young
Adults

By Ronald E. Hudkins

Description

As a teen or young adult picking your way forward through understanding financial investments, this book is specifically designed for you! It is written in a straightforward language and is a reliable resource that examines the fundamentals of mutual fund investing.

More and more people are looking into mutual funds to have a steady source of interest income, to save, or to help fund their retirement. In contrast to other forms of investment, mutual funds are always professionally managed by a financial expert in order to make sure that returns are maximized.

Interested in learning more? This book will provide a detailed explanation of mutual funds and how to manage them in simple layman's terms that even a beginning investor can understand. You will have an understanding of the Pros and Cons of Mutual Funds. You will learn about the different types of Mutual Funds such as Money Market, Bond Funds and Stock Funds.

Securing your financial future has never appeared more difficult than in today's turbulent market environment. After studying this book you will most likely be a better investor for having read this Common Sense roadmap to understanding the basics of Mutual Funds.

So, if you're interested in portfolio diversification you will likely be investing in mutual funds. As such, this book offers timeless advice in building your investment portfolio. It will provide you with expert insight on how to find the best-managed funds that match your financial goals. It will help you avoid fund-investing pitfalls and maximize your chances of success.

Investing (like many things) is all about common sense. This book should be in every career counselor's office and delivered to every teen or young adult as it contains savvy financial advice for today's street-smart young investors. It is filled with in-depth insights and practical basic advice. The financial lingo and clear explanations allow this book to be easily digested by a novice

Financial Disclaimer

The Content is intended only as a base reference to help you make financial decisions. It is broad in scope and does not consider your personal financial situation. Your personal financial situation is unique and the information and advice may not be appropriate for your situation. Accordingly, before making any final decisions or implementing any financial strategy, I recommend that you obtain additional information and advice of your accountant and other financial advisors who are fully aware of your individual circumstances.

You are advised to undertake your Due diligence by investigating any business or person prior to signing a contract.

You should consider this your legal obligation and as such apply it to your voluntary investigations. A common example of due diligence in various industries is the process through which a potential acquirer evaluates a target company or its assets before an acquisition. The theory behind due diligence thus holds that performing this type of investigation contributes significantly to informed decision making by enhancing the amount and quality of information available to you the decision maker. You should ensure that the information gathered is systematically used to deliberate in a reflexive manner on the decision(s) at hand and all information factors in the costs, benefits, and risks you anticipate to undertake.

DEDICATION

I dedicate this book to teens and young adults looking for sound advice on how to make smart financial choices needed to establish a firm footing as you work your way through school and the post-graduation years.

Just remember as your speeding down that new found road of freedom that how you spend your 20's financially will ultimately define you.

After all is said and done you should also know; after you get married, someone should know how to write a check correctly, save and invest. Because, even if you have tons of love, there's still going to be a lot of bills!

Table of Contents

Introduction

Over the past decade, American investors increasingly have turned to mutual funds to save for retirement and other financial goals. Mutual funds can offer the advantages of diversification and professional management. But, as with other investment choices, investing in mutual funds involves risk. And fees and taxes will diminish a fund's returns. It pays to understand both the upsides and downsides of mutual fund investing and how to choose products that match your goals and tolerance for risk.

This beginner's guide explains the basics of mutual fund investing, how mutual funds work, what factors to consider before investing, and how to avoid common pitfalls.

It is compiled mainly by using the guidance from the U.S. Securities and Exchange Commission, Office of Investor Education and Advocacy, 100 F Street, NE Washington, DC 20549-0213. You can call them Toll-free: (800) 732-0330 or visit their Website: www.investor.gov

Mutual fund Overview

This section is about mutual funds in the United States. For other forms of mutual investment, see investment fund.

The examples and perspective in this article **deal primarily with the United States and do not represent a worldwide view of the subject**. Please improve this article and discuss the issue on the talk page. *(September 2011)*

A **mutual fund** is a professionally managed investment fund that pools money from many investors to purchase securities.[1] While there is no legal definition of the term "mutual fund", it is most commonly applied only to those collective investment vehicles that are regulated and sold to the general public. They are sometimes referred to as "investment companies" or "registered investment companies". Hedge funds are not mutual funds, primarily because they cannot be sold to the general public.

In the United States, mutual funds must be registered with the U.S. Securities and Exchange Commission, overseen by a board of directors or board of trustees, and managed by a Registered Investment Advisor. Mutual funds are subject to an extensive and detailed regulatory regime set forth in the Investment Company Act of 1940. Mutual funds are not taxed on their income and profits if they comply with certain requirements under the U.S. Internal Revenue Code.

Mutual funds have both advantages and disadvantages compared to direct investing in individual securities. Today they play an important role in household finances, most notably in retirement planning.

There are three types of U.S. mutual funds— open-end funds, unit investment trusts, and closed-end funds. The most common type, open-end funds, must be willing to buy back shares from investors every business day. Exchange-traded funds (ETFs) are open-end funds or unit investment trusts that trade on an exchange. Non-exchange-traded open-end funds are most common, but ETFs have been gaining in popularity.

Mutual funds are generally classified by their principal investments. The four main categories of funds are money market funds, bond or fixed income funds, stock or equity funds, and hybrid funds. Funds may also be categorized as index (or passively managed) or actively managed.

Investors in a mutual fund pay the fund's expenses, which reduce the fund's returns and performance. There is controversy about the level of these expenses.

Structure

In the United States, a mutual fund is registered with the Securities and Exchange Commission (SEC). Open-end and closed-end funds are overseen by a board of directors (if organized as a corporation) or board of trustees (if organized as a trust). The Board is charged with ensuring that the fund is managed in the best interests of the fund's investors and with hiring the fund manager and other service providers to the fund.

The sponsor or fund management company, often referred to as the fund manager, trades (buys and sells) the fund's investments in accordance with the fund's investment objective. A fund manager must be a registered investment adviser. Funds that are managed by the same company under the same brand are known as a fund family or fund complex.

Mutual funds are not taxed on their income and profits as long as they comply with requirements established in the U.S. Internal Revenue Code. Specifically, they must diversify their investments, limit ownership of voting securities, distribute most of their income (dividends, interest, and capital gains net of losses) to their investors annually, and earn most of the income by investing in securities and currencies.[2] There is an exception: net losses incurred by a mutual fund are not distributed or passed through to fund investors but are retained by the fund to be able to offset future gains.

The characterization of a fund's income is unchanged when it is paid to shareholders. For example, when a mutual fund distributes dividend income to its shareholders, fund investors will report the distribution as dividend income on their tax return. As a result, mutual funds are often called "pass-through" vehicles, because they simply pass on income and related tax liabilities to their investors.

Mutual funds may invest in many kinds of securities. The types of securities that a particular fund may invest in are set forth in the fund's prospectus, a legal document which describes the fund's investment objective, investment approach and permitted investments. The investment objective describes the type of income that the fund seeks. For example, a capital appreciation fund generally looks to earn most of its returns from increases in the prices of the securities it holds, rather than from dividend or interest income. The investment approach describes the criteria that the fund manager uses to select investments for the fund.

A mutual fund's investment portfolio is continually monitored by the fund's portfolio manager or managers.

Hedge funds are not considered a type of (unregistered) mutual fund. While hedge funds are another type of collective investment vehicle, they are not governed by the Investment Company Act of 1940 and are not required to register with the SEC (though hedge fund managers must register as investment advisers).

Advantages and disadvantages

Mutual funds have advantages over investing directly in individual securities:[3]

- Increased diversification: A fund normally holds many securities; diversification decreases risk.

- Daily liquidity: Shareholders of open-end funds and unit investment trusts may sell their holdings back to the fund at the close of every trading day at a price equal to the closing net asset value of the fund's holdings.

- Professional investment management: Open-and closed-end funds hire portfolio managers to supervise the fund's investments.

- Ability to participate in investments that may be available only to larger investors. For example, individual investors often find it difficult to invest directly in foreign markets.

- Service and convenience: Funds often provide services such as check writing.

- Government oversight: Mutual funds are regulated by the SEC

- Ease of comparison: All mutual funds are required to report the same information to investors, which makes them easy to compare.

Mutual funds have disadvantages as well, which include:[4]

- Fees
- Less control over timing of recognition of gains
- Less predictable income
- No opportunity to customize

History

The first mutual funds were established in Europe. One researcher credits a Dutch merchant with creating the first mutual fund in 1774.[5]

Mutual funds were introduced to the United States in the 1890s, and they became popular in the 1920s.[5] These early funds were generally closed-end funds with a fixed number of shares that often traded at prices above the portfolio value.[6]

The first open-end mutual fund, called the Massachusetts Investors Trust (now part of the MFS family of funds), with redeemable shares was established on March 21, 1924. However, closed-end funds remained more popular than open-end funds throughout the 1920s. In 1929, open-end funds accounted for only 5% of the industry's $27 billion in total assets.[7]

After the stock market crash of 1929, Congress passed a series of acts regulating the securities markets in general and mutual funds in particular. The Securities Act of 1933 requires that all investments sold to the public, including mutual funds, be registered with the SEC and that they provide prospective investors with a prospectus that discloses essential facts about the investment. The Securities and Exchange Act of 1934 requires that issuers of securities, including mutual funds, report regularly to their investors; this act also created the Securities and Exchange Commission, which is the principal regulator of mutual funds. The Revenue Act of 1936 established guidelines for the taxation of mutual funds, while the Investment Company Act of 1940 governs their structure.

When confidence in the stock market returned in the 1950s, the mutual fund industry began to grow again. By 1970, there were approximately 360 funds with $48 billion in assets.[8] The introduction of money market funds in the high interest rate environment of the late 1970s boosted industry growth dramatically. The first retail index fund, First Index Investment Trust, was formed in 1976 by The Vanguard Group, headed by John Bogle; it is now called the "Vanguard 500 Index Fund" and is one of the world's largest mutual funds, with more than $195 billion in assets as of January 31, 2015.[9]

Fund industry growth continued into the 1980s and 1990s, as a result of three factors: a bull market for both stocks and bonds, new product introductions (including tax-exempt bond, sector, international and target date funds) and wider distribution of fund shares.[10] Among the new distribution channels were retirement plans. Mutual funds are now the preferred investment option in certain types of fast-growing retirement plans, specifically in 401(k) and other defined contribution plans and in individual retirement accounts (IRAs), all of which surged in popularity in the 1980s. Total mutual fund assets fell in 2008 as a result of the credit crisis of 2008.

In 2003, the mutual fund industry was involved in a scandal involving unequal treatment of fund shareholders. Some fund management companies allowed favored investors to engage in late trading, which is illegal, or market timing, which is a practice prohibited by fund policy. The scandal was initially discovered by former New York Attorney General Eliot Spitzer and led to a significant increase in regulation.

At the end of 2014, there were over 15,000 mutual funds in the United States with combined assets of $18.2 trillion, according to the Investment Company Institute (ICI), a trade association of U.S. investment companies. The ICI reports that worldwide mutual fund assets were $33.4 trillion on the same date.[11]

Mutual funds play an important role in U.S. household finances; by the end of 2014, funds accounted for 24% of household financial assets. Their role in retirement planning is particularly significant. Roughly half of the assets in 401(k) (and similar

retirement) plans and in individual
retirement accounts were invested in mutual
funds.[11]

Leading complexes

As of September 2015, the top ten open-end
fund managers in North America were:[12]

1. The Vanguard Group

2. Fidelity Investments

3. American Funds (Capital Group)

4. JPMorgan Chase

5. T. Rowe Price

6. BlackRock

7. Franklin Templeton Investments

8. PIMCO

9. Dimensional Fund Advisors

Types

There are three principal types of mutual
funds in the United States: open-end funds,
unit investment trusts (UITs); and closed-
end funds. Exchange-traded funds (ETFs) are

open-end funds or unit investment trusts that trade on an exchange; they have gained in popularity recently. ETFs are one type of "exchange-traded product". While the term "mutual fund" may refer to all three types of registered investment companies, it is more commonly used to refer exclusively to the open-and closed-end funds.There are two types of Mutual Funds in India, Equity Mutual Funds, and Debt Mutual Funds.[13]

Open-end funds

Main article: Open-end fund

Open-end mutual funds must be willing to buy back their shares from their investors at the end of every business day at the net asset value (NAV) computed that day. Most open-end funds also sell shares to the public every day; these shares are also priced at NAV. A professional investment manager oversees the portfolio, buying and selling securities as appropriate. The total investment in the fund will vary based on share purchases, share redemptions and fluctuation in market valuation. There is no legal limit on the number of shares that can be issued.

Open-end funds are the most common type of mutual fund. At the end of 2014, there were 7,923 open-end mutual funds in the United States with combined assets of $15.9 trillion.[11]

Closed-end funds

Main article: Closed-end fund

Closed-end funds generally issue shares to the public only once, when they are created through an initial public offering. Their shares are then listed for trading on a stock exchange. Investors who no longer wish to invest in the fund cannot sell their shares back to the fund (as they can with an open-end fund). Instead, they must sell their shares to another investor in the market; the price they receive may be significantly different from NAV. It may be at a "premium" to NAV (i.e., higher than NAV) or, more commonly, at a "discount" to NAV (i.e., lower than NAV). A professional investment manager oversees the portfolio, buying and selling securities as appropriate.

At the end of 2014, there were 568 closed-end funds in the United States with combined assets of $289 billion.[11]

Unit investment trusts

Main article: *Unit investment trust*

Unit investment trusts (UITs) can only issue to the public once, when they are created. UITs generally have a limited life span, established at creation. Investors can redeem shares directly with the fund at any time (similar to an open-end fund) or wait to redeem them upon the trust's termination. Less commonly, they can sell their shares in the open market. Unit investment trusts do not have a professional investment manager; their portfolio of securities is established at the UIT's creation and does not change.

At the end of 2014, there were 5,381 UITs in the United States with combined assets of $101 billion.[11]

Exchange-traded funds

Main article: *Exchange-traded fund*

A relatively recent innovation, exchange-traded funds (ETFs) are structured as open-end investment companies or UITs. ETFs are part of a larger category of investment vehicles known as "exchange-traded products" (ETPs), which, other than ETFs, may be structured as a partnership or grantor trust or may take the form of an exchange-traded note. Non-ETF exchange-traded products may be used to provide exposure to currencies and commodities.

ETFs combine characteristics of both closed-end funds and open-end funds. ETFs are traded throughout the day on a stock exchange. An arbitrage mechanism is used to keep the trading price close to net asset value of the ETF holdings.

Most ETFs are passively managed index funds, though actively managed ETFs are becoming more common.

ETFs have been gaining in popularity. At the end of 2014, there were 1,411 ETFs in the United States with combined assets of $2.0 trillion.[11]

Investments and classification

Mutual funds are normally classified by their principal investments, as described in the prospectus and investment objective. The four main categories of funds are money market funds, bond or fixed income funds, stock or equity funds and hybrid funds. Within these categories, funds may be subclassified by investment objective, investment approach or specific focus.

The SEC requires that mutual fund names be consistent with a fund's investments. For example, the "ABC New Jersey Tax-Exempt Bond Fund" would generally have to invest, under normal circumstances, at least 80% of its assets in bonds that are exempt from federal income tax, from the alternative minimum tax and from taxes in the state of New Jersey.[14]

Bond, stock, and hybrid funds may be classified as either index (passively managed) funds or actively managed funds.

Money market funds

Main article: Money market fund

Money market funds invest in money market instruments, which are fixed income securities with a very short time to maturity and high credit quality. Investors often use money market funds as a substitute for bank savings accounts, though money market funds are not insured by the government, unlike bank savings accounts.

Money market funds strive to maintain a $1.00 per share net asset value, meaning that investors earn interest income from the fund but do not experience capital gains or losses. If a fund fails to maintain that $1.00 per share because its securities have declined in value, it is said to "break the buck". Only two money market funds have ever broken the buck—Community Banker's U.S. Government Money Market Fund in 1994 and the Reserve Primary Fund in 2008.

In 2014, the SEC approved significant changes in money market fund regulation. Beginning in October 2016, money market funds that are sold to institutional investors and that invest in non-government securities will no longer be allowed to maintain a stable $1.00 per share net asset value. Instead, these funds will be required to have a floating net asset value.

At the end of 2014, money market funds accounted for 17% of open-end fund assets.[11]

Bond funds

Main article: *Bond fund*

Bond funds invest in fixed income or debt securities. Bond funds can be subclassified according to the specific types of bonds owned (such as high-yield or junk bonds, investment-grade corporate bonds, government bonds or municipal bonds) and by the maturity of the bonds held (short-, intermediate- or long-term). Bond funds may invest in primarily U.S. securities (domestic or U.S. funds), in both U.S. and foreign securities (global or world funds), or primarily foreign securities (international funds).

At the end of 2014, bond funds accounted for 22% of open-end fund assets.[11]

Stock funds

Main article: *Stock fund*

Stock or equity funds invest in common stocks which represent an ownership share (or equity) in corporations. Stock funds may invest in primarily U.S. securities (domestic or U.S. funds), in both U.S. and foreign securities (global or world funds), or primarily foreign securities (international funds). They may focus on a specific industry or sector.

A stock fund may be subclassified along two dimensions: (1) market capitalization and (2) investment style (i.e., growth vs. blend/core vs. value). The two dimensions are often displayed in a grid known as a "style box".

Market capitalization ("cap") indicates the size of the companies in which a fund invests, based on the value of the company's stock. Each company's market capitalization equals the number of shares outstanding times the market price of the stock. Market capitalizations are typically divided into the following categories, with approximate market capitalizations in parentheses:

- Micro cap (below $300 million)
- Small cap (below $2 billion)
- Mid cap
- Large cap (at least $10 billion)

Funds can also be classified in these categories based on the market caps of the stocks that it holds.

Stock funds are also subclassified according to their investment style: growth, value, or blend (or core). Growth funds seek to invest in stocks of fast-growing companies. Value funds seek to invest in stocks that appear cheaply priced. Blend funds are not biased toward either growth or value.

At the end of 2014, stock funds accounted for 52% of the assets in all U.S. mutual funds.[11]

Hybrid funds

Hybrid funds invest in both bonds and stocks or in convertible securities. Balanced funds, asset allocation funds, target date or target risk funds and lifecycle or lifestyle funds are all types of hybrid funds.

Hybrid funds may be structured as funds of funds, meaning that they invest by buying shares in other mutual funds that invest in securities. Many fund of funds invest in affiliated funds (meaning mutual funds managed by the same fund sponsor), although some invest in unaffiliated funds (i.e., managed by other fund sponsors) or some combination of the two.

At the end of 2014, hybrid funds accounted for 9% of the assets in all U.S. mutual funds.[11]

Index (passively managed) versus actively managed

Main articles: Index fund and active management

An index fund or passively managed fund seeks to match the performance of a market index, such as the S&P 500 index, while an actively managed fund seeks to outperform a relevant index through superior security selection.

Expenses

Investors in a mutual fund pay the fund's expenses. These expenses fall into five categories: distribution charges (sales loads and 12b-1 fees), the management fee, securities transaction fees, shareholder transaction fees and fund services charges. Some of these expenses reduce the value of an investor's account; others are paid by the fund and reduce net asset value.

Recurring fees and expenses—specifically the 12b-1 fee, the management fee and other fund expenses—are included in a fund's total expense ratio (TER), often referred to simply the "expense ratio". Because all funds must compute an expense ratio using the same method, investors may compare costs across funds.

There is considerable controversy about the level of mutual fund expenses.

Management fee

Main article: Management fee

The management fee is paid to the Management Company or sponsor that organizes the fund, provides the portfolio management or investment advisory services and normally lends its brand to the fund. The fund manager may also provide other administrative services. The management fee often has breakpoints, which means that it declines as assets (in either the specific fund or in the fund family as a whole) increase. The management fee is paid by the fund and is included in the expense ratio.

The fund's board reviews the management fee annually. Fund shareholders must vote on any proposed increase, but the fund manager or sponsor can agree to waive some or all of the management fee in order to lower the fund's expense ratio.

Distribution charges

Main article: Mutual fund fees and expenses

Distribution charges pay for marketing, distribution of the fund's shares as well as services to investors. There are three types of distribution charges:

- Front-end load or sales charge. A front-end load or sales charge is a commission paid to a broker by a mutual fund when shares are purchased. It is expressed as a percentage of the total amount invested or the "public offering price", which equals the net asset value plus the front-end load per share. The front-end load often declines as the amount invested increases, through breakpoints. The front-end load is paid by the shareholder; it is deducted from the amount invested.

- Back-end load. Some funds have a back-end load, which is paid by the investor when shares are redeemed. If the back-end load declines the longer the investor holds shares, it is called a contingent deferred sales charges (CDSC). Like the front-end load, the back-end load is paid by the shareholder; it is deducted from the redemption proceeds.

- 12b-1 fees. Some funds charge an annual fee to compensate the distributor of fund shares for providing ongoing services to fund shareholders. This fee is called a 12b-1 fee, after the SEC rule authorizing it. The 12b-1 fee is paid by the fund and reduces net asset value.

A no-load fund does not charge a front-end load or back-end load under any circumstances and does not charge a 12b-1 fee greater than 0.25% of fund assets.

Securities transaction fees

A mutual fund pays expenses related to buying or selling the securities in its portfolio. These expenses may include brokerage commissions. Securities transaction fees increase the cost basis of investments purchased and reduce the proceeds from their sale. They do not flow through a fund's income statement and are not included in its expense ratio. The amount of securities transaction fees paid by a fund is normally positively correlated with its trading volume or "turnover".

Shareholder transaction fees

Shareholders may be required to pay fees for certain transactions. For example, a fund may charge a flat fee for maintaining an individual retirement account for an investor. Some funds charge redemption fees when an investor sells fund shares shortly after buying them (usually defined as within 30, 60 or 90 days of purchase); redemption fees are computed as a percentage of the sale amount. Shareholder transaction fees are not part of the expense ratio.

Fund services charges

A mutual fund may pay for other services including:

- Board of directors or trustees fees and expenses

- Custody fee: paid to a custodian bank for holding the fund's portfolio in safekeeping and collecting income owed on the securities

- Fund administration fee: for overseeing all administrative affairs such as preparing financial statements and shareholder reports, SEC filings, monitoring compliance, computing total returns and other performance information, preparing/filing tax returns and all expenses of maintaining compliance with state blue sky laws

- Fund accounting fee: for performing investment or securities accounting services and computing the net asset value (usually every day the New York Stock Exchange is open)

- Professional services fees: legal and auditing fees

- Registration fees: paid to the SEC and state securities regulators

- Shareholder communications expenses: printing and mailing required documents to shareholders such as shareholder reports and prospectuses

- Transfer agent service fees and expenses: for keeping shareholder records, providing statements and tax forms to investors and providing telephone, internet and or other investor support and servicing

- Other/miscellaneous fees

The fund manager or sponsor may agree to subsidize some of these other expenses in order to lower the fund's expense ratio.

Controversy

Critics of the fund industry argue that fund expenses are too high. They believe that the market for mutual funds is not competitive and that there are many hidden fees, so that it is difficult for investors to reduce the fees that they pay. They argue that the most effective way for investors to raise the returns they earn from mutual funds is to invest in funds with low expense ratios.

Fund managers counter that fees are determined by a highly competitive market and, therefore, reflect the value that investors attribute to the service provided. They also note that fees are clearly disclosed.

Share classes

A single mutual fund may give investors a choice of different combinations of front-end loads, back-end loads and 12b-1 fees, by offering several different types of shares, known as share classes. All of them invest in the same portfolio of securities, but each has different expenses and, therefore, a different net asset value and different performance results. Some of these share classes may be available only to certain types of investors.

Funds offering multiple classes often identify them with letters, though they may also use names such as "Investor Class", "Service Class", "Institutional Class", etc., to identify the type of investor for which the class is intended. The SEC does not regulate the names of share classes, so that specifics of a share class with the same name may vary from fund family to fund family.

Typical share classes for funds sold through brokers or other intermediaries are as follows:

- **Class A** shares usually charge a front-end sales load together with a small 12b-1 fee.

- **Class B** shares usually do not have a front-end sales load; rather, they have a high contingent deferred sales charge (CDSC) that gradually declines over several years, combined with a high 12b-1 fee. Class B shares usually convert automatically to Class A shares after they have been held for a certain period.

- **Class C** shares usually have a high 12b-1 fee and a modest contingent deferred sales charge that is discontinued after one or two years. Class C shares usually do not convert to another class. They are often called "level load" shares.

- **Class I** are usually subject to very high minimum investment requirements and are, therefore, known as "institutional" shares. They are no-load shares.

- **Class R** are usually for use in retirement plans such as 401(k) plans. They typically do not charge loads, but do charge a small 12b-1 fee.

No-load funds often have two classes of shares:

- **Class I** shares do not charge a 12b-1 fee

- **Class N** shares charge a 12b-1 fee of no more than 0.25% of fund assets

Neither class of shares typically charges a front-end or back-end load

Definitions

Definitions of key terms.

Net asset value

Main article: Net asset value

A fund's net asset value (NAV) equals the current market value of a fund's holdings minus the fund's liabilities (sometimes referred to as "net assets"). It is usually expressed as a per-share amount, computed by dividing net assets by the number of fund shares outstanding. Funds must compute their net asset value according to the rules set forth in their prospectuses. Funds compute their NAV at the end of each day that the New York Stock Exchange is open, though some funds compute NAVs more than once daily.

Valuing the securities held in a fund's portfolio is often the most difficult part of calculating net asset value. The fund's board typically oversees security valuation.

Expense ratio]

The expense ratio allows investors to compare expenses across funds. The expense ratio equals the 12b-1 fee plus the management fee plus the other fund expenses divided by average daily net assets. The expense ratio is sometimes referred to as the total expense ratio (TER).

Average annual total return

The SEC requires that mutual funds report the average annual compounded rates of return for one-, five-and ten year-periods using the following formula:[15]

$P(1+T)^n = ERV$

Where:

P = a hypothetical initial payment of $1,000

T = average annual total return

n = number of years

ERV = ending redeemable value of a hypothetical $1,000 payment made at the beginning of the one-, five-, or ten-year periods at the end of the one-, five-, or ten-year periods (or fractional portion)

Turnover

Turnover is a measure of the volume of a fund's securities trading. It is expressed as a percentage of average market value of the portfolio's long-term securities. Turnover is the lesser of a fund's purchases or sales during a given year divided by average long-term securities market value for the same period. If the period is less than a year, turnover is generally annualized.

Overview References

1. *"U.S. Securities and Exchange Commission Information on Mutual Funds"*. *U.S. Securities and Exchange Commission (SEC). Retrieved 2011-04-06.*

2. *"26 U.S. Code § 851 – Definition of regulated investment company"*. *Legal Information Institute. Cornell University Law School. Retrieved 9 March 2015. 851(b)(2) and (3)*

3. *Pozen, Robert; Hamacher, Theresa (2014). The Fund Industry: How Your Money is Managed (Second Edition). John Wiley & Sons. pp. 4–5.*

4. Pozen and Hamacher (2014), pp. 7–8.

5. ^ Jump up to: *a* *b* K. Geert Rouwenhorst (December 12, 2004), "The Origins of Mutual Funds", Yale ICF Working Paper No. 04-48.

6. *Fink, Matthew P. (2008). The Rise of Mutual Funds. Oxford University Press. p. 9.*

7. Fink (2008), p. 15.

8. Fink (2008), p. 63.

9. *"Vanguard – 500 Index Fund Investor Shares". The Vanguard Group. Retrieved 2015-02-18.*

10.   Pozen and Hamacher (2014), pp. 10–14.

11.   ^ Jump up to: *a b c d e f g h i i 2015 Investment Company Fact Book. Investment Company Institute. Retrieved 2 November 2015.*

12.   EY Global Fund Distribution

13.   *Jain, Pulkit. "types". Mutual Fund Income. Legalraasta.*

14.   17 CFR 270.35d-1

15.   *"Final Rule: Registration Form Used by Open-End Management Investment Companies: Sample Form and instructions". U.S. Securities and*

Exchange Commission (SEC).
Retrieved 2008-09-25.

External links

- U.S. Securities and Exchange Commission's Guide for Mutual Fund Investors

Further reading

- *Matthew P. Fink (2011). The Rise of Mutual Funds: An Insider's View (2nd ed.). Oxford University Press. ISBN 978-0199753505.*

- *Robert Pozen; Theresa Hamacher (2015). The Fund Industry: How Your Money is Managed (2nd ed.). Hoboken, NJ: Wiley Finance. ISBN 978-1118929940.*

Chapter One

An Overview of Mutual Funds

Some Key Points to Remember

• Mutual funds are **not** guaranteed or insured by the FDIC or any other government agency — even if you buy through a bank and the fund carries the bank's name. You can lose money investing in mutual funds.

• Past performance is not a reliable indicator of future performance. So don't be dazzled by last year's high returns. But past performance can help you assess a fund's volatility over time.

• All mutual funds have costs that lower your investment returns. Shop around, and use a mutual fund cost calculator at www.sec.gov/investor/tools.shtml to compare many of the costs of owning different funds *before* you buy.

How Mutual Funds Work

What They Are

A mutual fund is a company that pools money from many investors and invests the money in stocks, bonds, short-term money-market instruments, other securities or assets, or some combination of these investments. The combined holdings the mutual fund owns are known as its portfolio. Each share represents an investor's proportionate ownership of the fund's holdings and the income those holdings generate.

Other Types of Investment Companies

Legally known as an "open-end company," a mutual fund is one of three basic types of investment companies. While this brochure discusses **only** mutual funds, you should be aware that other pooled investment vehicles exist and may offer features that you desire. The two other basic types of investment companies are:

Closed-end funds — which, unlike mutual funds, sell a fixed number of shares at one time (in an initial public offering) that later trade on a secondary market; and

Unit Investment Trusts (UITs) — which make a one-time public offering of only a specific, fixed number of redeemable securities called "units" and which will terminate and dissolve on a date specified at the creation of the UIT.

"Exchange-traded funds" (ETFs) are a type of investment company that aims to achieve the same return as a particular market index. They can be either open-end companies or UITs. But ETFs are not considered to be, and are not permitted to call themselves, mutual funds.

Some of the traditional, distinguishing characteristics of mutual funds include the following:

➤	Investors purchase mutual fund shares from the fund itself (or through a broker for the fund) instead of from other investors on a secondary market, such as the New York Stock Exchange or Nasdaq Stock Market.
➤	The price that investors pay for mutual fund shares is the fund's per share net asset value (NAV) plus any shareholder fees that the fund imposes at the time of purchase (such as sales loads).
➤	Mutual fund shares are "redeemable," meaning investors can sell their shares back to the fund (or to a broker acting for the fund).
➤	Mutual funds generally create and sell new shares to accommodate new investors. In other words, they sell their shares on a continuous basis, although some funds stop selling when, for example, they become too large.

> The investment portfolios of mutual funds typically are managed by separate entities known as "investment advisers" that are registered with the SEC.

A Word About Hedge Funds and "Funds of Hedge Funds"

"Hedge fund" is a general, non-legal term used to describe private, unregistered investment pools that traditionally have been limited to sophisticated, wealthy investors. Hedge funds are *not* mutual funds and, as such, are *not* subject to the numerous regulations that apply to mutual funds for the protection of investors — including regulations requiring a certain degree of liquidity, regulations requiring that mutual fund shares be redeemable at any time, regulations protecting against conflicts of interest, regulations to assure fairness in the pricing of fund shares, disclosure regulations, regulations limiting the use of leverage, and more.

"Funds of hedge funds," a relatively new type of investment product, are investment companies that invest in hedge funds. Some, but not all, register with the SEC and file semi-annual reports. They often have lower minimum investment thresholds than traditional, unregistered hedge funds and can sell their shares to a larger number of investors. Like hedge funds, funds of hedge funds are not mutual funds. Unlike open-end mutual funds, funds of hedge funds offer very limited rights of redemption. And, unlike ETFs, their shares are not typically listed on an exchange.

You'll find more information about hedge funds on our website. To learn more about funds of hedge funds, please read FINRA's Investor Alert entitled Funds of Hedge Funds: Higher Costs and Risks for Higher Potential Returns.

Advantages and Disadvantages

Every investment has advantages and disadvantages. But it's important to remember that features that matter to one investor may not be important to you. Whether any particular feature is an advantage for you will depend on your unique circumstances. For some investors, mutual funds provide an attractive investment choice because they generally offer the following features:

- **Professional Management** — Professional money managers research, select, and monitor the performance of the securities the fund purchases.

- **Diversification** — Diversification is an investing strategy that can be neatly summed up as "Don't put all your eggs in one basket." Spreading your investments across a wide range of companies and industry sectors can help lower your risk if a company or sector fails. Some investors find it easier to achieve diversification through ownership of mutual funds rather than through ownership of individual stocks or bonds.

- **Affordability** — some mutual funds accommodate investors who don't have a lot of money to invest by setting relatively low dollar amounts for initial purchases, subsequent monthly purchases, or both.

- **Liquidity** — Mutual fund investors can readily redeem their shares at the current NAV — plus any fees and charges assessed on redemption — at any time.

But mutual funds also have features that some investors might view as disadvantages, such as:

- **Costs Despite Negative Returns** — Investors must pay sales charges, annual fees, and other expenses (which we'll discuss below) regardless of how the fund performs. And, depending on the timing of their investment, investors may also have to pay taxes on any capital gains distribution they receive — even if the fund went on to perform poorly after they bought shares.

- **Lack of Control** — Investors typically cannot ascertain the exact make-up of a fund's portfolio at any given time, nor can they directly influence which securities the fund manager buys and sells or the timing of those trades.

- **Price Uncertainty** — with an individual stock, you can obtain real-time (or close to real-time) pricing information with relative ease by checking financial websites or by calling your broker. You can also monitor how a stock's price changes from hour to hour — or even second to second. By contrast, with a mutual fund, the price at which you purchase or redeem shares will typically depend on the fund's NAV, which the fund might not calculate until many hours after you've placed your order. In general, mutual funds must calculate their NAV at least once every business day, typically after the major U.S. exchanges close.

Different Types of Funds

When it comes to investing in mutual funds, investors have literally thousands of choices. Before you invest in any given fund, decide whether the investment strategy and risks of the fund are a good fit for you. The first step to successful investing is figuring out your financial goals and risk tolerance — either on your own or with the help of a financial professional. Once you know what you're saving for, when you'll need the money, and how much risk you can tolerate, you can more easily narrow your choices.

Most mutual funds fall into one of three main categories — money market funds, bond funds (also called "fixed income" funds), and stock funds (also called "equity" funds). Each type has different features and different risks and rewards. Generally, the higher the potential return, the higher the risk of loss.

Money Market Funds

Money market funds have relatively low risks, compared to other mutual funds (and most other investments). By law, they can invest in only certain high-quality, short-term investments issued by the U.S. government, U.S. corporations, and state and local governments. Money market funds try to keep their net asset value (NAV) — which represents the value of one share in a fund — at a stable $1.00 per share. But the

NAV may fall below $1.00 if the fund's investments perform poorly. Investor losses have been rare, but they are possible.

Money market funds pay dividends that generally reflect short-term interest rates, and historically the returns for money market funds have been lower than for either bond or stock funds. That's why "inflation risk" — the risk that inflation will outpace and erode investment returns over time — can be a potential concern for investors in money market funds.

Bond Funds

Bond funds generally have higher risks than money market funds, largely because they typically pursue strategies aimed at producing higher yields. Unlike money market funds, the SEC's rules do not restrict bond funds to high-quality or short-term investments. Because there are many different types of bonds, bond funds can vary dramatically in their risks and rewards. Some of the risks associated with bond funds include:

Credit Risk — the possibility that companies or other issuers whose bonds are owned by the fund may fail to pay their debts (including the debt owed to holders of their bonds). Credit risk is less of a factor for bond funds that invest in insured bonds or U.S. Treasury bonds. By contrast, those that invest in the bonds of companies with poor credit ratings generally will be subject to higher risk.

Interest Rate Risk — the risk that the market value of the bonds will go down when interest rates go up. Because of this, you can lose money in any bond fund, including those that invest only in insured bonds or Treasury bonds. Funds that invest in longer-term bonds tend to have higher interest rate risk.

Prepayment Risk — the chance that a bond will be paid off early. For example, if interest rates fall, a bond issuer may decide to pay off (or "retire") its debt and issue new bonds that pay a lower rate. When this happens, the fund may not be able to reinvest the proceeds in an investment with as high a return or yield.

Stock Funds

Although a stock fund's value can rise and fall quickly (and dramatically) over the short term, historically stocks have performed better over the long term than other types of investments — including corporate bonds, government bonds, and treasury securities.

Overall "market risk" poses the greatest potential danger for investors in stocks funds. Stock prices can fluctuate for a broad range of reasons — such as the overall strength of the economy or demand for particular products or services.

Not all stock funds are the same. For example:

- *Growth* funds focus on stocks that may not pay a regular dividend but have the potential for large capital gains.

- *Income* funds invest in stocks that pay regular dividends.

- *Index* funds aim to achieve the same return as a particular market index, such as the S&P 500 Composite Stock Price Index, by investing in all — or perhaps a representative sample — of the companies included in an index.

- *Sector* funds may specialize in a particular industry segment, such as technology or consumer products stocks.

How to Buy and Sell Shares

You can purchase shares in some mutual funds by contacting the fund directly. Other mutual fund shares are sold mainly through brokers, banks, financial planners, or insurance agents. All mutual funds will redeem (buy back) your shares on any business day and must send you the payment within seven days.

The easiest way to determine the value of your shares is to call the fund's toll-free number or visit its website. The financial pages of major newspapers sometimes print the NAVs for various mutual funds. When you buy shares, you pay the current NAV per share plus any fee the fund assesses at the time of purchase, such as a purchase sales load or other type of purchase fee. When you sell your shares, the fund will pay you the NAV minus any fee the fund assesses at the time of redemption, such as a deferred (or back-end) sales load or redemption fee. A fund's NAV goes up or down daily as its holdings change in value.

Exchanging Shares

A "family of funds" is a group of mutual funds that share administrative and distribution systems. Each fund in a family may have different investment objectives and follow different strategies.

Some funds offer exchange privileges within a family of funds, allowing shareholders to transfer their holdings from one fund to another as their investment goals or tolerance for risk change. While some funds impose fees for exchanges, most funds typically do not. To learn more about a fund's exchange policies, call the fund's toll-free number, visit its website, or read the "shareholder information" section of the prospectus.

Bear in mind that exchanges have tax consequences. Even if the fund doesn't charge you for the transfer, you'll be liable for any capital gain on the sale of your old shares — or, depending on the circumstances, eligible to take a capital loss. We'll discuss taxes in further detail below.

How Funds Can Earn Money for You

You can earn money from your investment in three ways:

- **Dividend Payments** — A fund may earn income in the form of dividends and interest on the securities in its portfolio. The fund then pays its shareholders nearly all of the income (minus disclosed expenses) it has earned in the form of dividends.

- **Capital Gains Distributions** — The price of the securities a fund owns may increase. When a fund sells a security that has increased in price, the fund has a capital gain. At the end of the year, most funds distribute these capital gains (minus any capital losses) to investors.

- **Increased NAV** — If the market value of a fund's portfolio increases after deduction of expenses and liabilities, then the value (NAV) of the fund and its shares increases. The higher NAV reflects the higher value of your investment.

With respect to dividend payments and capital gains distributions, funds usually will give you a choice: the fund can send you a check or other form of payment, or you can have your dividends or distributions *reinvested* in the fund to buy more shares (often without paying an additional sales load).

Factors to Consider

Thinking about your long-term investment strategies and tolerance for risk can help you decide what type of fund is best suited for you. But you should also consider the effect that fees and taxes will have on your returns over time.

Degrees of Risk

All funds carry some level of risk. You may lose some or all of the money you invest — your principal — because the securities held by a fund go up and down in value. Dividend or interest payments may also fluctuate as market conditions change.

Before you invest, be sure to read a fund's prospectus and shareholder reports to learn about its investment strategy and the potential risks. Funds with higher rates of return may take risks that are beyond your comfort level and are inconsistent with your financial goals.

A Word About Derivatives

Derivatives are financial instruments whose performance is derived, at least in part, from the performance of an underlying asset, security, or index. Even small market movements can dramatically affect their value, sometimes in unpredictable ways.

There are many types of derivatives with many different uses. A fund's prospectus will disclose whether and how it may use derivatives. You may also want to call a fund and ask how it uses these instruments.

Fees and Expenses

As with any business, running a mutual fund involves costs — including shareholder transaction costs, investment advisory fees, and marketing and distribution expenses. Funds pass along these costs to investors by imposing fees and expenses. It is important that you understand these charges because they lower your returns.

Some funds impose "shareholder fees" directly on investors whenever they buy or sell shares. In addition, every fund has regular, recurring, fund-wide "operating expenses." Funds typically pay their operating expenses out of fund assets — which means that investors indirectly pay these costs.

SEC rules require funds to disclose both shareholder fees and operating expenses in a "fee table" near the front of a fund's prospectus. The lists below will help you decode the fee table and understand the various fees a fund may impose:

Shareholder Fees

- **Sales Charge (Load) on Purchases** — the amount you pay when you buy shares in a mutual fund. Also known as a "front-end load," this fee typically goes to the brokers that sell the fund's shares. Front-end loads reduce the amount of your investment. For example, let's say you have $1,000 and want to invest it in a mutual fund with a 5% front-end load. The $50 sales load you must pay comes off the top, and the remaining $950 will be invested in the fund. According to FINRA rules, a front-end load cannot be higher than 8.5% of your investment.

- **Purchase Fee** — another type of fee that some funds charge their shareholders when they buy shares. Unlike a front-end sales load, a purchase fee is paid to the fund (not to a broker) and is typically imposed to defray some of the fund's costs associated with the purchase.

- **Deferred Sales Charge (Load)** — a fee you pay when you sell your shares. Also known as a "back-end load," this fee typically goes to the brokers that sell the fund's shares. The most common type of back-end sales load is the "contingent deferred sales load" (also known as a "CDSC" or "CDSL"). The amount of this type of load will depend on how long the investor holds his or her shares and typically decreases to zero if the investor holds his or her shares long enough.

- **Redemption Fee** — another type of fee that some funds charge their shareholders when they sell or redeem shares. Unlike a deferred sales load, a redemption fee is paid to the fund (not to a broker) and is typically used to defray fund costs associated with a shareholder's redemption.

- **Exchange Fee** — a fee that some funds impose on shareholders if they exchange (transfer) to another fund within the same fund group or "family of funds."

- **Account fee** — a fee that some funds separately impose on investors in connection with the maintenance of their accounts. For example, some funds impose an account maintenance fee on accounts whose value is less than a certain dollar amount.

Annual Fund Operating Expenses

- **Management Fees** — fees that are paid out of fund assets to the fund's investment adviser for investment portfolio management, any other management fees payable to the fund's investment adviser or its affiliates, and administrative fees payable to the investment adviser that are not included in the "Other Expenses" category (discussed below).

- **Distribution [and/or Service] Fees ("12b-1" Fees)** — fees paid by the fund out of fund assets to cover the costs of marketing and selling fund shares and sometimes to cover the costs of providing shareholder services. "Distribution fees" include fees to compensate brokers and others who sell fund shares and to pay for advertising, the printing and mailing of prospectuses to new investors, and the printing and mailing of sales literature. "Shareholder Service Fees" are fees paid to persons to respond to investor inquiries and provide investors with information about their investments.

- **Other Expenses** — expenses not included under "Management Fees" or "Distribution or Service (12b-1) Fees," such as any shareholder service expenses that are not already included in the 12b-1 fees, custodial expenses, legal and accounting expenses, transfer agent expenses, and other administrative expenses.

- **Total Annual Fund Operating Expenses ("Expense Ratio")** — the line of the fee table that represents the total of all of a fund's annual fund operating expenses, expressed as a percentage of the fund's average net assets. Looking at the expense ratio can help you make comparisons among funds.

A Word About "No-Load" Funds

Some funds call themselves "no-load." As the name implies, this means that the fund does not charge any type of sales load. But, as discussed above, not every type of shareholder fee is a "sales load." A no-load fund may charge fees that are not sales loads, such as purchase fees, redemption fees, exchange fees, and account fees. No-load funds will also have operating expenses.

Be sure to review carefully the fee tables of any funds you're considering, including no-load funds. Even small differences in fees can translate into large differences in returns over time. For example, if you invested $10,000 in a fund that produced a 10% annual return before expenses and had annual operating expenses of 1.5%, then after 20 years you would have roughly $49,725. But if the fund had expenses of only 0.5%, then you would end up with $60,858 — an 18% difference.

A mutual fund cost calculator can help you understand the impact that many types of fees and expenses can have over time. It takes only minutes to compare the costs of different mutual funds.

A Word About Breakpoints

Some mutual funds that charge front-end sales loads will charge lower sales loads for larger investments. The investment levels required to obtain a reduced sales load are commonly referred to as "breakpoints."

The SEC does not require a fund to offer breakpoints in the fund's sales load. But, if breakpoints exist, the fund must disclose them. In addition, a FINRA member brokerage firm should not sell you shares of a fund in an amount that is "just below" the fund's sales load breakpoint simply to earn a higher commission.

Each fund company establishes its own formula for how they will calculate whether an investor is entitled to receive a breakpoint. For that reason, it is important to seek out breakpoint information from your financial advisor or the fund itself. You'll need to ask how a particular fund establishes eligibility for breakpoint discounts, as well as what the fund's breakpoint amounts are. FINRA's Mutual Fund Breakpoint HYPERLINK "http://www.sec.gov/cgi-bin/goodbye.cgi?www.nasd.com/fundsearch" Search Tool can help you determine whether you're entitled to breakpoint discounts.

Classes of Funds

Many mutual funds offer more than one class of shares. For example, you may have seen a fund that offers "Class A" and "Class B" shares. Each class will invest in the same "pool" (or investment portfolio) of securities and will have the same investment objectives and policies. But each class will have different shareholder services and/or distribution arrangements with different fees and expenses. As a result, each class will likely have different performance results.

A multi-class structure offers investors the ability to select a fee and expense structure that is most appropriate for their investment goals (including the time that they expect to remain invested in the fund). Here are some key characteristics of the most common mutual fund share classes offered to individual investors:

- **Class A Shares** — Class A shares typically impose a front-end sales load. They also tend to have a lower 12b-1 fee and lower annual expenses than other mutual fund share classes. Be aware that some mutual funds reduce the front-end load as the size of your investment increases. If you're considering Class A shares, be sure to inquire about breakpoints.

- **Class B Shares** — Class B shares typically do not have a front-end sales load. Instead, they may impose a contingent deferred sales load and a 12b-1 fee (along with other annual expenses). Class B shares also might convert automatically to a class with a lower 12b-1 fee if the investor holds the shares long enough.

- **Class C Shares** — Class C shares might have a 12b-1 fee, other annual expenses, and either a front- or back-end sales load. But the front- or back-end load for Class C shares tends to be lower than for Class A or Class B shares, respectively. Unlike Class B shares, Class C shares generally do not convert to another class. Class C shares tend to have higher annual expenses than either Class A or Class B shares.

Tax Consequences

When you buy and hold an individual stock or bond, you must pay **income tax** each year on the dividends or interest you receive. But you won't have to pay any **capital gains**

tax until you actually sell and unless you make a profit.

Mutual funds are different. When you buy and hold mutual fund shares, you will owe income tax on any ordinary dividends in the year you receive or reinvest them. And, in addition to owing taxes on any *personal capital gains* when you sell your shares, you may also have to pay taxes each year on *the fund's capital gains*. That's because the law requires mutual funds to distribute capital gains to shareholders if they sell securities for a profit that can't be offset by a loss.

Tax Exempt Funds

If you invest in a tax-exempt fund — such as a municipal bond fund — some or all of your dividends will be exempt from federal (and sometimes state and local) income tax. You will, however, owe taxes on any capital gains.

Bear in mind that if you receive a capital gains distribution, you will likely owe taxes — even if the fund has had a negative return from the point during the year when you purchased your shares. For this reason, you should call the fund to find out when it makes distributions so you won't pay more than your fair share of taxes. Some funds post that information on their websites.

SEC rules require mutual funds to disclose in their prospectuses after-tax returns. In calculating after-tax returns, mutual funds must use standardized formulas similar to the ones used to calculate before-tax average annual total returns. You'll find a fund's after-tax returns in the "Risk/Return Summary" section of the prospectus. When comparing funds, be sure to take taxes into account.

Avoiding Common Pitfalls

If you decide to invest in mutual funds, be sure to obtain as much information about the fund *before* you invest. And don't make assumptions about the soundness of the fund based solely on its past performance or its name.

Sources of Information

Prospectus

When you purchase shares of a mutual fund, the fund *must* provide you with a prospectus. But you can — and should — request and read a fund's prospectus *before* you invest. The prospectus is the fund's selling document and contains valuable information, such as the fund's investment objectives or goals, principal strategies for achieving those goals, principal risks of investing in the fund, fees and expenses, and past performance. The prospectus also identifies the fund's managers and advisers and describes how to purchase and redeem fund shares.

While they may seem daunting at first, mutual fund prospectuses contain a treasure trove of valuable information. The SEC requires funds to include specific categories of information in their prospectuses and to present key data (such as fees and past performance) in a standard format so that investors can more easily compare different funds.

Here's some of what you'll find in mutual fund prospectuses:

- **Date of Issue** — The date of the prospectus should appear on the front cover. Mutual funds must update their prospectuses at least once a year, so always check to make sure you're looking at the most recent version.

- **Risk/Return Bar Chart and Table —** Near the front of the prospectus, right after the fund's narrative description of its investment objectives or goals, strategies, and risks, you'll find a **bar chart** showing the fund's annual total returns for each of the last 10 years (or for the life of the fund if it is less than 10 years old). All funds that have had annual returns for at least one calendar year must include this chart.

  Except in limited circumstances, funds also must include a **table** that sets forth returns — both before and after taxes — for the past 1-, 5-, and 10-year periods. The table will also include the returns of an appropriate broad-based index for comparison purposes.

Here's what the table will look like:

	1-year	5-year (or life of fund)	10-year (or life of fund)
Return before taxes	____%	____%	____%
Return after taxes on distributions	____%	____%	____%
Return after taxes on distributions and sale of fund shares	____%	____%	____%
***Index* (reflects no deductions for [fees, expenses, or taxes])**	____%	____%	____%

Note: Be sure to read any footnotes or accompanying explanations to make sure that you fully understand the data the fund provides in the bar chart and table. Also, bear in mind that the bar chart and table for a multiple-class fund (that offers more than one class of fund shares in the prospectus) will typically show performance data and returns for *only one* class.

- **Fee Table** — following the performance bar chart and annual returns table, you'll find a table that describes the fund's fees and expenses. These include the shareholder fees and annual fund operating expenses described in greater detail above. The fee table includes an example that will help you compare costs among different funds by showing you the costs associated with investing a hypothetical $10,000 over a 1-, 3-, 5-, and 10-year period.

- **Financial Highlights** — This section, which generally appears towards the back of the prospectus, contains audited data concerning the fund's financial performance for each of the past 5 years. Here you'll find net asset values (for both the beginning and end of each period), total returns, and various ratios, including the ratio of expenses to average net assets, the ratio of net income to average net assets, and the portfolio turnover rate.

Profile

Some mutual funds also furnish investors with a "profile," which summarizes key information contained in the fund's prospectus, such as the fund's investment objectives, principal investment strategies, principal risks, performance, fees and expenses, after-tax returns, identity of the fund's investment adviser, investment requirements, and other information.

Statement of Additional Information ("SAI")

Also known as "Part B" of the registration statement, the SAI explains a fund's operations in greater detail than the prospectus — including the fund's financial statements and details about the history of the fund, fund policies on borrowing and concentration, the identity of officers, directors, and persons who control the fund, investment advisory and other services, brokerage commissions, tax matters, and performance such as yield and average annual total return information. If you ask, the fund must send you an SAI. The back cover of the fund's prospectus should contain information on how to obtain the SAI.

Shareholder Reports

A mutual fund also must provide shareholders with annual and semi-annual reports within 60 days after the end of the fund's fiscal year and 60 days after the fund's fiscal mid-year. These reports contain a variety of updated financial information, a list of the fund's portfolio securities, and other information. The information in the shareholder reports will be current as of the date of the particular report (that is, the last day of the fund's fiscal year for the annual report, and the last day of the fund's fiscal mid-year for the semi-annual report).

Investors can obtain all of these documents by:

➤	Calling or writing to the fund (all mutual funds have toll-free telephone numbers);
➤	Visiting the fund's website;
➤	Contacting a broker that sells the fund's shares;
➤	Searching the SEC's EDGAR database and downloading the documents for free; or
➤	Accessing "How to Request Public Documents".

Past Performance

A fund's past performance is not as important as you might think. Advertisements, rankings, and ratings often emphasize how well a fund has performed in the past. But studies show that the future is often different. This year's "number one" fund can easily become next year's below average fund.

Be sure to find out how long the fund has been in existence. Newly created or small funds sometimes have excellent short-term performance records. Because these funds may invest in only a small number of stocks, a few successful stocks can have a large impact on their performance. But as these funds grow larger and increase the number of stocks they own, each stock has less impact on performance. This may make it more difficult to sustain initial results.

While past performance does not necessarily predict future returns, it *can* tell you how volatile (or stable) a fund has been over a period of time. Generally, the more volatile a fund, the higher the investment risk. If you'll need your money to meet a financial goal in the near-term, you probably can't afford the risk of investing in a fund with a volatile history because you will not have enough time to ride out any declines in the stock market.

Looking Beyond a Fund's Name

Don't assume that a fund called the "XYZ Stock Fund" invests **only** in stocks or that the "Martian High-Yield Fund" invests **only** in the securities of companies headquartered on the planet Mars. The SEC requires that any mutual fund with a name suggesting that it focuses on a particular type of investment must invest at least 80% of its assets in the type of investment suggested by its name. But funds can still invest up to one-fifth of their holdings in other types of securities — including securities that you might consider too risky or perhaps not aggressive enough.

Bank Products versus Mutual Funds

Many banks now sell mutual funds, some of which carry the bank's name. But mutual funds sold in banks, including money market funds, are *not* bank deposits. As a result, they are *not* federally insured by the Federal Deposit Insurance Corporation (FDIC).

Money Market Matters

Don't confuse a "money market fund" with a "money market deposit account." The names are similar, but they are completely different:

- A money market fund is a type of mutual fund. It *is not* guaranteed or FDIC insured. When you buy shares in a money market fund, you should receive a prospectus.

> - A money market deposit account is a bank deposit. It *is* guaranteed and FDIC insured. When you deposit money in a money market deposit account, you should receive a Truth in Savings form.

If You Have Problems If you encounter a problem with your mutual fund, you can send us your complaint using our online complaint form. You can also reach us by regular mail at:

Securities and Exchange Commission
Office of Investor Education and Advocacy
100 F Street, N.E.
Washington, D.C. 20549-0213

> We have provided this information as a service to investors. It is neither a legal interpretation nor a statement of SEC policy. If you have questions concerning the meaning or application of a particular law or rule, please consult with an attorney who specializes in securities law.

Ref1 Chapter One – Mutual Funds Overview courtesy of Article titled - Invest Wisely: An Introduction to Mutual Funds posted by the U.S. Securities and Exchange Commission, November 2015 @ http://www.sec.gov/investor/pubs/inwsmf.htm

Chapter Two

Calculating Mutual Fund Fees and Expenses

Fees and expenses are an important consideration in selecting a mutual fund because these charges lower your returns. Many investors find it helpful to compare the fees and expenses of different mutual funds before they invest.

You can compare the fees and expenses of up to three mutual funds, or the share classes of the same mutual fund on the FINRA's Mutual Fund Expense Analyzer. You can also compare the fees and expenses of up to three ETFs using the same tool.

With just some basic information, you can use the tool to compare the costs of different mutual funds in a manner of seconds. That's because the tool automatically provides fee and expense information for you. Simply enter each fund's ticker symbol or select the fund through the drop down menu. If you can't remember the full name of the fund, you can also search for the fund using key words.

A mutual fund's fees and expenses may be more important than you realize. Advertisements, rankings, and ratings often emphasize how well a fund has performed in the past. But studies show that the future is often different. This year's "number one" fund can easily become next year's below average fund. On the other hand, independent studies show fees and expenses can be a reliable predictor of mutual fund performance.

Of course, selecting a mutual fund involves more than just picking one with low fees and expenses. Before you invest in any mutual fund, decide whether the investment goals and risks of the fund are a good fit for you and determine how it will affect the diversification of your entire portfolio. You can read about a fund's goals, risks, and costs in its prospectus.

Ref2 Chapter Two - courtesy of Article titled - Calculating Mutual Fund Fees and Expenses posted by the U.S. Securities and Exchange Commission, November 2015 @ http://www.sec.gov/investor/tools/mfcc/mfcc-int.htm

Chapter Three

Breakpoint Discounts

Everyone knows that buying in bulk can save money. The same principle applies to buying mutual fund shares. Some mutual funds that charge front-end sales loads will reduce those fees for larger investments. For example, a fund might charge a 5% front-end sales load for investments up to $25,000, but reduce that to a 4% load for investments between $25,000 and $50,000 and 3% for investments exceeding $50,000. The investment levels required to obtain a reduced sales load – in this case, $25,000 and $50,000 – are commonly referred to as "breakpoints." Funds are not required to offer breakpoint discounts and those that do may set them at their discretion.

A fund that offers breakpoint discounts must not only disclose the breakpoints, but must also alert investors to the availability of breakpoint discounts, in its prospectus. In addition, a brokerage firm that is a member of the Financial Industry Regulatory Authority (FINRA) is prohibited from selling to investors shares of a fund in a dollar amount just below one of the fund's breakpoints, thus depriving investors of a discount, so as to earn a higher commission.

Each fund company has its own formula for how it will calculate whether an investor is entitled to receive a breakpoint discount. Some funds determine eligibility for a breakpoint discount by looking at total investments in the fund by household, which may include multiple accounts, such as retirement savings accounts and college savings accounts. Others look only at the total amount that an individual has invested personally. Fund investors may also be entitled to combine prior fund purchase amounts to obtain a breakpoint discount on additional investments in the fund. Some funds permit investors to obtain a breakpoint discount if the investors agree to make additional purchases in the future. In such cases, the investor signs a "letter of intent" to make additional purchases in the future, and the failure to honor that pledge may result in retroactive fees that rescind the discount.

Investors should always check to make sure that they get any breakpoint discounts they are entitled to receive. Investors who believe they have not received breakpoint discounts to which they are entitled should first contact their broker or the fund company that sold them the fund and request the discount. If the issue isn't resolved to the investor's satisfaction, he or she should ask for a written response from the broker or the fund company. If the investor is not satisfied with the response, he or she has the right to file a complaint with the SEC using our online complaint form.

Ref3 Chapter Three - courtesy of Article titled - Breakpoint Discounts posted by the U.S. Securities and Exchange Commission, November 2015 @
http://www.sec.gov/answers/breakpt.htm

Chapter Four

Avoiding Common Pitfalls

If you decide to invest in mutual funds, be sure to obtain as much relevant information as possible about the fund before you invest. And don't make assumptions about the soundness of the fund based solely on its past performance or its name.

SOURCES OF INFORMATION

Prospectus

When you purchase shares of a mutual fund, the fund must provide you with a prospectus. But you can and should request and read a fund's prospectus before you invest. The prospectus is the fund's selling document and contains valuable information, such as the fund's investment objectives or goals, principal strategies for achieving those goals, principal risks of investing in the fund, fees and expenses, and past performance. The prospectus also identifies the fund's managers and advisers and describes how to purchase and redeem fund shares. While they may seem daunting at first, mutual fund prospectuses contain a treasure trove of valuable information. The SEC requires funds to include specific categories of information in their prospectuses and to present key data (such as fees and past performance) in a standard format so that investors can more easily compare different funds. Here's some of what you'll find in mutual fund prospectuses:

•Date of Issue—

The date of the prospectus should appear on the front cover. Mutual funds must update their prospectuses at least once a year, so always check to make sure you're looking at the most recent version.

•Risk/Return Bar Chart and Table—

Near the front of the prospectus, right after the fund's narrative description of its investment objectives or goals, strategies, and risks, you'll find a bar chart showing the fund's annual total returns for each of the last 10 years (or for the life of the fund if it is less than 10 years old). All funds that have had annual returns for at least one calendar year must include this chart.

Except in limited circumstances, funds also must include a table that sets forth returns—both before and after taxes—for the past 1-,

5-, and 10-year periods. The table will also include the returns of an appropriate broad-based index for comparison purposes.

Note: Be sure to read any footnotes or accompanying explanations to make sure that you fully understand the data the fund provides in the bar chart and table. Also, bear in mind that the bar chart and table for a multiple-class fund (that offers more than one class of fund shares in the prospectus) will typically show performance data and returns for only one class.

•Fee Table—

Following the performance bar chart and annual returns table, you'll find a table that describes the fund's fees and expenses.

These include the shareholder fees and annual fund operating expenses described in greater detail (on pages). The fee table includes an example that will help you compare costs among different funds by showing you the costs associated with investing a hypothetical $10,000 over a 1-, 3-, 5-, and➤10-yearperiod.

•Financial   Highlights—

This section, which generally appears towards the back of the prospectus, contains audited data concerning the fund's financial performance for each of the past 5 years.

MUTUAL FUNDS

Here you'll find net asset values (for both the beginning and end of each period), total returns, and various ratios, including the ratio of expenses to average net assets, the ratio of net income to average net assets, and the portfolio turnover rate.

Profile Some mutual funds also furnish investors with a "profile," which summarizes key information contained in the fund's prospectus, such as the fund's investment objectives, principal investment strategies, principal risks, performance, fees and expenses, after-tax returns, identity of the fund's investment adviser, investment requirements, and other information.

Statement of Additional Information ("SAI") Also known as "Part B" of the registration statement, the SAI explains a fund's operations in greater detail than the prospectus—including the fund's financial statements and details about the history of the fund, fund policies on borrowing and concentration, the identity of officers, directors, and persons who control the fund, investment advisory and other services, brokerage commissions, tax matters, and performance such as yield and average annual total return information. If you ask, the fund must send you an SAI. The back cover of the fund's prospectus should contain information on how to obtain the SAI.

Shareholder Reports A mutual fund also must provide shareholders with annual and semiannual reports within 60 days after the end of the fund's fiscal year and 60 days after the fund's fiscal mid-year. These reports contain a variety of updated financial information, a list of the fund's portfolio securities, and other information. The information in the shareholder reports will be current as of the date of the particular report (that is, the last day of the fund's fiscal year for the annual report, and the last day of the fund's fiscal mid-year for the semi-annual report).

A GUIDE FOR INVESTORS

Investors can obtain all of these documents by:

Calling or writing to the fund (all mutual funds have toll-free telephone numbers);

 Visiting the fund's website;

Contacting a broker that sells the fund's shares;

Searching the SEC's EDGAR database at http://www.sec.gov/ edgar.shtml and downloading the documents for free; or

Contacting the SEC's Office of Investor Education and Advocacy by telephone at (202) 551-8090, by fax at (202) 772-9295, or by email at publicinfo@sec.gov. Please be aware that we charge a per page fee for photocopying.

PAST PERFORMANCE

A fund's past performance is not as important as you might think. Advertisements, rankings, and ratings often emphasize how well a fund has performed in the past. But studies show that the future is often different. This year's "number one" fund can easily become next year's below average fund. Be sure to find out how long the fund has been in existence. Newly created or small funds sometimes have excellent short-term performance records. Because these funds may invest in only a small number of stocks, a few successful stocks can have a large impact on their performance. But as these funds grow larger and increase the number of stocks they own, each stock has less impact on performance. This may make it more difficult to sustain initial results. While past performance does not necessarily predict future returns, it can tell you how volatile (or stable) a fund has been over a period of time. Generally, the more volatile a fund, the higher the investment risk. If you'll need your money to meet a financial goal in the near-term, you probably can't afford the risk of investing in a fund with a volatile history because you will not have enough time to ride out any declines in the stock market.

MUTUAL FUNDS

LOOKING BEYOND A FUND'S NAME

Don't assume that a fund called the "XYZ Stock Fund" invests only in stocks or that the "Martian High-Yield Fund" invests only in the securities of companies headquartered on the planet Mars. The SEC requires that any mutual fund with a name suggesting that it focuses on a particular type of investment must invest at least 80% of its assets in the type of investment suggested by its name. But funds can still invest up to one fifth of their holdings in other types of securities— including securities that you might consider too risky or perhaps not aggressive enough.

BANK PRODUCTS VERSUS MUTUAL FUNDS

Many banks now sell mutual funds, some of which carry the bank's name. But mutual funds sold in banks, including money market funds, are not bank deposits. As a result, they are not federally insured by the Federal Deposit Insurance Corporation (FDIC).

MONEY MARKET MATTERS

Don't confuse a "money market fund" with a "money market deposit account." The names are similar, but they are completely different:

• A money market fund is a type of mutual fund. It is not guaranteed or FDIC insured. When you buy shares in a money market fund, you should receive a prospectus.

• A money market deposit account is a bank deposit. It is guaranteed and FDIC insured. When you deposit money in a money market deposit account, you should receive a Truth in Savings form.

Ref4 Chapter Four - Avoiding Common Pitfalls courtesy of Publication titled – Mutual Funds, A Guide for Investors posted by the U.S. Securities and Exchange Commission, November 2015 @ https://www.sec.gov/investor/pubs/sec-guide-to-mutual-funds.pdf

Chapter Five

Transferring Your Brokerage Account:

Tips on Avoiding Delays

Many investors transfer their accounts from one brokerage firm to another without a hitch. If your transfer goes smoothly, count on the whole process taking two to three weeks. But this time frame may vary depending upon such factors as the assets involved, the types of accounts, and the institutions between which the transfer occurs.

Transfers may be delayed if:

- The wrong transfer form is used;
- The transfer form has been incorrectly completed;
- The transfer involves a request to liquidate some or all of your assets;
- The transfer includes a margin account;
- The transfer is from one type of account into a different type of account;
- A change in the account owner is made; or

- The transfer involves a retirement account.

This document walks you through the transfer process and provides tips on how to avoid problems.

Use the Right Form

Use the correct form to ensure your transfer goes smoothly. Some firms allow you to use one form for all account transfers while others have different forms depending on the type of account you are transferring (for example, an IRA account or a margin account). To get the right form, call the new firm where you want to transfer your account or visit its Web site.

Review the Form Carefully

As you start filling in the transfer form, review the account statement from your old firm where your account is held. All firms require you to attach a copy of your most recent account statement to the transfer form.

The form usually asks for the name on your account, the type of account you want to transfer, account number, the firm where the account is held, and your social security or tax identification number. Be sure you provide this information exactly as it appears on your old account. For instance, if your middle name or initial appears on your old account, you may run into delays if you forget to include it. When transferring only some of the securities in your account, carefully list the securities you want to transfer on the form.

The easiest way to transfer your account is to keep the type of accounts the same (joint account transfers to joint account; IRA to IRA) and account owner the same. You can change account type or ownership at the time of the transfer, but this may delay the transfer. You may need to provide documents proving changes to ownership, such as a marriage certificate, divorce decree, or death certificate.

If you have questions about how to complete the form, contact the new firm for help. Once completed, keep a copy of the form for your records.

Understand the Transfer Process

All transfers start and end with your new firm, but your old firm needs to take action too.

Electronic Transfers

Most account transfers between brokerage firms are made using the Automated Customer Account Transfer Service (or "ACATS") system. The National Securities Clearing Corporation operates ACATS, and both the New York Stock Exchange and the National Association of Securities Dealers, Inc. require their member firms to use ACATS.

These rules require firms to complete various stages of the transfer process within a limited period of time. If the transfer is made through ACATS, and there are no problems, the transfer should take no more than six business days to complete from the time your new firm enters your form into ACATS.

During this time, your old firm compares the information you provided on the transfer form with its information. If the information matches, your old and new firms review the transferable assets. If the transfer includes a margin account, the new firm also examines the account to see whether the account meets the firm's margin standards. Firms may have different margin standards about how much they will lend you to trade. While the transfer is in progress, your account may be "frozen" for part of the time. If this occurs, you may be unable to trade. Check with both your old and new firms if you want to trade during the transfer process.

Under the "ACATS for Banks" program initiated by DTCC in February 1999, banks may voluntarily participate in ACATS. If a bank participates in the program, then a transfer from the participating bank to a brokerage firm or vice a versa should occur in the standard ACATS time frame of six business days. If you are transferring your account to or from a bank you should ask whether the bank participates in the "ACATS for Banks" program.

Be aware that delays may occur when you transfer a retirement account. Because retirement accounts require a financial institution, such as a bank, to act as the custodian or holder of the account, you must have a custodial arrangement in place at your new financial institution before the transfer can occur. A delay may happen if you have not paid the maintenance fee to the old custodian or the new custodian does not allow a security in the retirement account to be transferred. Once everything is in place, the transfer can be made through ACATS.

Manual Transfers

Sometimes, a transfer is made manually. This occurs when your assets are with a bank, mutual fund, credit union, insurance company, or limited partnership that does not participate in ACATS. This also may occur if you request a liquidation of assets other than the standard money market fund in your account. There are no set time frames for completing a manual transfer with these financial institutions. For that reason - and the potential risk of market volatility should there be any delay - you may not want to liquidate any assets via instructions on the transfer form.

A manual transfer may also occur when you request a partial transfer of your account between brokerage firms. The rules of the NYSE and FINRA require firms to expedite or complete these requests in a reasonable amount of time, but firms have the option to make these transfers electronically through ACATS. If you are making a partial transfer, tell the new firm you would like the transfer to go through ACATS.

Monitor Your Transfer

Since both the old and new firms must act to complete the transfer, stay in touch with both of them. Make sure the new firm has received your transfer form. If you sent the form to a branch office, it may take a few days before it is received at the firm's headquarters for processing.

You may also want to ask the old firm whether it has received the transfer request. If the transfer goes through ACATS, the old firm has three business days from the time it receives the transfer form to decide if it is going to complete or reject the transfer. If the assets in an account can be transferred through ACATS, a firm can reject a transfer request only if the form has been completed incorrectly or there is a question about the ownership of the account or the number of shares. Ask the firm whether it will transfer your account or if there is a problem with your instructions. If there is a problem, ask for an explanation and how to correct it.

If the old firm takes no action on the request or a problem is not resolved within six business days, the transfer request is purged (or deleted) from ACATS. If that happens, the new firm must start over by again inputting the transfer request into ACATS.

Know Which Securities May Not Transfer

Some types of securities may not be transferred. These securities include:

- Securities sold exclusively by your old firm;
- Mutual funds or money market funds not available at the new firm;
- Limited partnerships that are private placements;
- Annuities; or
- Bankrupt securities.

If your request includes some of these non-transferable securities, it may take longer to complete a transfer. Your old firm is required to transfer whatever securities or assets it can through ACATS and ask you what you want to do with the others. You generally have two choices: either sell the non-transferable security and transfer the cash, or leave the security with your old firm. Sometimes, you may be able to take possession of the security itself. Taking possession of a security may pose risks, such as the security could be stolen. Also, it may not be advisable for retirement plans.

Keep These Final Thoughts in Mind

Your old firm may charge you a fee for the transfer to cover administrative costs. Sometimes, the new firm will also charge a fee. These fees are typically spelled out in your account agreements with the firms.

Expect delays in receiving dividends, interest, and proceeds from sales of securities. They often arrive at your old firm after the transfer has taken place. Your old firm is required to transfer them to you at your new firm — within ten business days of receipts — for at least six months after the account transfer is completed.

If you feel like your account has not been transferred in a timely fashion, ask to speak to the compliance director at your old or new firm. If you are not satisfied, contact the New York Stock Exchange or the FINRA, depending on where your brokerage firm is a member.

Finally, Ask Questions! A simple error could significantly delay the transfer. Be certain your old and new firms have the information they need to make the transfer happen in a timely fashion.

Ref5 Chapter Five - Transferring Your Brokerage Account: Tips on Avoiding Delays Investors posted by the U.S. Securities and Exchange Commission, November 2015 @ http://www.sec.gov/investor/pubs/acctxfer.htm

Chapter Six

Questions You Should Ask About Your Investments

That's the best advice we can give you about how to invest wisely. We see too many investors who might have avoided trouble and losses if they had asked basic questions from the start.

We encourage you to thoroughly evaluate the background of any financial professional with whom you intend to do business— *before* you hand over your hard-earned cash.

Investor Tip

Which financial professional you select is very important for several reasons. You'll want to investigate thoroughly before doing business with a financial professional or firm that has a history of complaints or problems with regulators. Also, you should know that if your financial professional or his or her firm goes out of

---

business or declares bankruptcy, you might not be able to recover your money—even if an arbitrator or a court rules in your favor.

It doesn't matter if you are a beginner or have been investing for many years, it's never too early or too late to start asking questions. It's almost impossible to ask a dumb question about how you are investing your money. Don't feel intimidated. Remember, it's your money at stake. You are paying for the assistance of a financial professional.

A good financial professional will welcome your questions, no matter how basic. Financial professionals know that an educated client is an asset, not a liability. They would rather answer your questions before you invest, than confront your anger and confusion later.

In this brochure, you'll find some questions that you should ask about investment products, the people who sell those products, and the people who provide investment advice to you. We've also included some tips on how to monitor your investments and handle any problems.

Keep this brochure on hand when considering an investment and use it by asking the right questions before you buy. Have a pen and piece of paper ready to take notes on the answers. They can come in handy if there is a dispute later about what was said during the transaction. Taking notes also sends a signal to your financial professional: I'm a smart and serious investor who wants to know more about the risks and rewards of investing.

Questions about Products:

Is this investment product registered with the SEC and my state securities agency?

Does this investment match my investment goals? Why is this investment suitable for me?

How will this investment make money? (Dividends? Interest? Capital gains?) Specifically, what must happen for this investment to increase in value? (For example, increase in interest rates, real estate values, or market share?)

What are the total fees to purchase, maintain, and sell this investment? Are there ways that I can reduce or avoid some of the fees that I'll pay, such as purchasing the investment directly? After all the fees are paid, how much does this investment have to increase in value before I break even?

How liquid is this investment? How easy would it be to sell if I needed my money right away?

What are the specific risks associated with this investment? What is the maximum I could lose? (For example, what will be the effect of changing interest rates, economic recession, high competition, or stock market ups and downs?)

How long has the company been in business? Is its management experienced? Has management been successful in the past? Have they ever made money for investors before?

Is the company making money? How are they doing compared to their competitors?

Where can I get more information about this investment? Can I get the latest reports filed by the company with the SEC: a prospectus or offering circular, or the latest annual report and financial statements?

For mutual funds:

How has this fund performed over the long run? Where can I get an independent evaluation of this fund?

What specific risks are associated with this fund?

What type of securities does the fund hold? How often does the portfolio change?

Does this mutual fund invest in any type of securities that could cause the value to go up or down rapidly in a short period of time? (For example, derivatives?)

How does the fund perform compared to other funds of the same type or to an index of the same type of investment?

How much will the fund charge me when I buy shares? What ongoing fees are charged? How much will the fund charge me when I sell shares?

Is the fund portable? If I move my assets to another firm, will I be able to continue holding the fund or will I need to liquidate it?

Questions About The People Who Sell Investments or Provide Investment Advice:

Are you registered with our state securities regulator? Have you ever been disciplined by the SEC, a state regulator, or other organization (such as NASD or one of the stock exchanges)?

Investor Tip - Check Out Your Financial Professional

You can verify your broker's disciplinary history by checking the Central Registration Depository (CRD). Either your state securities regulator or NASD can provide you with CRD

---

information. Your state securities regulator may give you more information from the CRD than NASD, especially when it comes to investor complaints, so you may want to check with them first. You'll find contact information for your state securities regulator on the website of the North American Securities Administrators Association. To contact FINRA, visit FINRA's BrokerCheck website, or call them toll-free at (800)289-9999.

You can find out about investment advisers and whether they are properly registered by reading their registration forms, called the "Form ADV." You can view an adviser's most recent Form ADV online by visiting the Investment Adviser Public Disclosure (IAPD) website. At present, the IAPD database contains Forms ADV only for investment adviser firms that register electronically using the Investment Adviser Registration

Depository. You can also get copies of Form ADV for individual advisers and firms from the investment adviser, your state securities regulator, or the SEC, depending on the size of the adviser.

How long has your firm been in business? How many arbitration awards have been filed against your firm?

What training and experience do you have? How long have you been in the business? What other firms have you been registered with? What is the status of those firms today?

Have you personally been involved in any arbitration cases? What happened?

What is your investment philosophy?

Describe your typical client. Can you provide me with some names and telephone numbers of your long term clients?

How do you get paid? By commission? Amount of assets you manage? Another method?

Do I have any choices on how to pay you? Should I pay you by the transaction? Or a flat fee regardless of how many transactions I have?

Do you make more if I buy this stock (or bond, or mutual fund) rather than another? If you weren't making extra money, would your recommendation be the same?

Are you participating in a sales contest? Is this purchase really in my best interest, or are you trying to win a prize?

You've told me what it costs me to buy this stock (or bond, or mutual fund); how much will I receive if I sell it today?

Where do you send my order to be executed? Can we get a better price if we send it to another market?

If your financial professional changes firms, ask: Did they pay you to change firms? Do you get anything for bringing me along?

Questions about the Progress of Your Investments:

How frequently do I get statements? Do I understand what the statement tells me?

Is the return on my investment meeting my expectations and goals? Is this investment performing as I was led to believe?

How much money will I get back if I sell my investment today?

How much am I paying in commission or fees?

Have my goals changed? If so, are my investments still suitable?

What criteria will I use to decide when to sell?

How to Handle Problems:

Act promptly! By law, you only have a limited time to take legal action. Follow these steps to solve your problem:

1. Talk to your financial professional and explain the problem. Where is the fault? Were communications clear? Refer to your notes. What did the financial professional tell you? What do your notes say?

2. If your financial professional can't resolve your problem, then talk to the financial professional's supervisor (which, for brokers, is often the firm's branch manager).

3. If the problem is still not resolved, write to the compliance department at the firm's main office. Explain your problem clearly, and how you want it resolved. Ask the compliance office to respond to you within 30 days. If you're still not satisfied:

4. Send us your complaint by using our online complaint form or you can reach us as follows:

Securities and Exchange Commission
Office of Investor Education and Advocacy
100 F Street, N.E.
Washington, D.C. 20549-0213

At the SEC, we will research your complaint, contact the firm or person you have complained about and ask them to respond to your specific complaint or question. Sometimes our intervention yields a satisfactory result. If these steps don't work, you may need to take legal action on your own. We can send you information on mediation and arbitration, and suggest how to locate a lawyer if you need one.

Investor Tip

When you ask these questions, write down the answers you receive and what you decided to do. If something goes wrong, your notes can help to establish what was said. Let your financial professional know you're taking notes. They'll know you're a serious investor and may tell you more. Use our form for taking notes when you speak to your financial professional.

For more information on how to invest wisely, ask for our publications: Invest Wisely: Advice From Your Securities Industry Regulators, Protect Your Money: Check Out Brokers and Investment Advisers, and Invest Wisely: An Introduction to Mutual Funds. You can also get other SEC publications online or by calling our toll-free publications line at (800) SEC-0330.

Ref6 Chapter Six - Questions You Should Ask about Your Investments and What to Do If You Run into Problems posted by the U.S. Securities and Exchange Commission, November 2015 @ http://www.sec.gov/investor/pubs/askquestions.htm

Chapter Seven

Don't Put All Your Apples in One Basket

Despite its recent declines, Apple stock is still up 543% since the market low of March 9, 2009. Even if you bought Apple last year, you still made a hefty 40% return. There is no denying that Apple has been a fantastic investment. Maybe you didn't purchase any Apple stock, so you think you missed out on a great opportunity. But whether you bought the stock or not, unbeknownst to you, you may actually own much more of that famous fruit than you think. Be careful, too many bites of Apple could make your financial stomach (portfolio) hurt if the stock continues to slide.

Watch Your Weight

Most investors use mutual funds to diversify and gain exposure to well-known indexes such as the S&P 500 or NASDAQ. Nearly all large cap funds boast having Apple as one of their top 10 holdings. It is true that these indexes offer the opportunity for diversification because of their broad based holdings, but because these indexes are market-cap weighted, their exposure (and your risk) to Apple grows every time Apple stock rises. Indexes are created in one of three ways: price weighted, market-cap weighted, or equal weighted. A price weighted index (i.e. Dow Jones Industrial Average) is heavily influenced by the highest priced stock in the index; a market-cap weighted index is heavily influenced by the largest company in that index; and an equal weighted index is adjusted periodically so that each component has an equal weight.

Many mutual funds and Exchange Traded Funds (ETF) that track the S&P 500 or NASDAQ have seen their exposure to Apple grow over time because most are market-cap weighted. For example, the Fidelity Contrafund (FCNTX) has seen its exposure to Apple grow from 6.9% in 2011 to 9.4% in 2012; the SPDR S&P 500 (SPY) went from having 2.7% of its assets in Apple to 4.4% in 2012; and PowerShares NASDAQ (QQQ) has nearly 18% of its assets in Apple, up from 15% in 2011. If you think you have sufficiently diversified by owning these large cap funds and have a few shares of Apple on the side, you may have too many Apples in your proverbial basket.

Don't Follow the Herd

Investors and actively managed mutual fund managers alike are known to follow the herd. Fund managers that do not have Apple stock in their top 10 holdings saw their judgment questioned by the fund's shareholders, similar to when Warren Buffett was questioned by shareholders as to why he would not buy dot.com stocks in the 1990s; Buffett was later vindicated for having avoided the dot.com bubble. During the dot-com era, it seemed everyone was investing in internet stocks. It wasn't uncommon to hear everyday investors at cocktail parties brag about their investments in Cisco, Lucent, AOL, and other venerable companies that subsequently lost tremendous value when the market collapsed. The people who lost the most in their retirement and investment accounts were those who became overly concentrated in a single sector or stock and failed to diversify out of those positions. They only realized after the fact that they were overexposed to technology stocks. Fast forward a few years, and these same individuals migrated to the next hottest investment – real estate. Many wrongly assumed that real estate would never lose value. After that came the gold craze, and most recently the Apple sensation. What's next? Facebook?

Use the 5% Rule

While it's a great feeling to see one of your stock picks skyrocket like Apple has, the reality is that not all of your stocks will be future winners. I always recommend that clients keep no more than 5% of their total portfolio in individual stocks because, while individual stocks can have tremendous growth potential, one bad stock can ruin your entire portfolio, especially if that one stock is a large part of your portfolio. No one expected such giant companies like Enron, Fannie Mae, General Motors, Lehman Brothers, AIG, Circuit City, Global Crossing, WorldCom, UAL Corp (parent of United Airlines), AOL, Lucent, etc. to either go bankrupt or completely wipe out their shareholders, but they did, and many people lost their entire life savings. Do not let yourself become overly exposed to one stock or sector of the market.

I am not attempting to predict the future price of Apple or advising against owning individual stocks altogether. I am simply reminding investors of the clear, but sometimes not-so-easy decision to review your portfolio periodically. Make sure you are not overly exposed to any segment of the market, and that you're not taking on more risk than you can handle.

Ref7 Chapter Seven – Financial Planning Association > Life Events > Catalog Item-796695515 @ http://www.plannersearch.org/life-events/financial-planning/investments/Don't%20Put%20All%20Your%20Apples%20in%20One%20Basket article written by Ara Oghoorian, CFA, CFP®

Chapter Eight

Common Investment Abuses

Everyone that hasn't been lost at sea for the past few years has heard of Bernie Madoff. What we typically see in the news are cases of outright fraud like Madoff's: Ponzi schemes, offshore scams, illegal promissory notes, etc. Investment abuses that are much more common, however, are cases where no criminal fraud has been committed. Many investors have been the victims of unscrupulous or incompetent practices on the part of a broker or investment adviser, and these are what we'll address today.

It's worth noting that every CFP® practitioner and Registered Investment Adviser must adhere to a fiduciary standard, which is much more stringent than the suitability standard that is enforced by FINRA and used as a guide by the great majority of the thousands of brokers it supervises. For more on the important differences between these standards of care, view the statement of the Financial Planning Coalition to Congress.

<u>Here are a few of the most common problems:</u>

<u>Misrepresentations and omissions.</u> A broker has a duty to fairly disclose all of the risks associated with an investment. If a brokerage firm misrepresents or omits material facts regarding an investment to you, and you subsequently lose money on that investment, the firm could be liable for damages.

<u>Unsuitable recommendations.</u> In making an investment recommendation to you, a broker must make recommendations that are consistent with your risk tolerance, financial needs and experience, and investment objectives. A broker has a duty to gather essential information in order to understand these factors, as well as the tax considerations, income needs, and the level of return desired. If a broker breaches those duties and makes unsuitable recommendations to you, the broker may be liable. So, for example, an advisor is making an unsuitable recommendation when he recommends that an elderly client of limited means, who requires capital preservation,

invest in a speculative investment.

Mutual fund and variable annuity sales
abuses. These include the unsuitable sale or
replacement of variable, equity-indexed or
fixed annuities, the sale of unsuitable mutual
fund share classes, or unsuitable switching of
mutual funds. Breakpoint selling is another
way for the broker to maximize
commissions: rather than use suitable funds
from the same fund family, the broker sells
you funds from multiple families to avoid
discounting sales charges. Learn more
about annuity abuses.

Over-concentration. Diversification is one of
the most important rules of investing, and
one of the best ways to control risk and
avoid excessive losses. If an advisor
concentrates too much of your portfolio into
one type of investment (or asset class), puts
too much of your money in only one or two
different stocks, or buys too many stocks in
the same industry, you face a much greater
risk of a large loss. A broker who does not
properly diversify your portfolio is potentially
liable if that investment declines in value.

Inappropriate use of margin. "Margin" trading is borrowing money from your broker to buy a stock and using your investment as collateral. Trading on margin increases your risk of loss for two reasons. First, the customer is at risk to lose more than the amount invested if the value of the security depreciates significantly. Second, the interest being charged to the account adds to the investors costs, thereby requiring the investments to appreciate even more to cover the cost of the interest before the customer realizes a net gain.

Excessive trading/churning. Churning occurs when a broker engages in excessive trading in an account in relation to your investment objectives. A commission-based broker may churn an account in an attempt to generate maximum commissions.

Unauthorized investments. When a broker purchases or sells a security in your non-discretionary account without your prior approval, the broker has engaged in unauthorized trading. A non-discretionary account requires customer contact and consent prior to the execution of each and every trade. A discretionary account does not, but must be opened with a separate authorization agreement.

Failure to follow instructions. A broker has a duty to follow your instructions regarding the entry and execution of orders, and failure to follow your instructions in a timely manner will violate industry rules.

Next month we'll examine how to take action if you suspect that you have been the victim of investment abuse. In the meantime, it is always worth having your investment accounts reviewed by a CERTIFIED FINANCIAL PLANNER™ professional from the Financial Planning Association (FPA).

Ref8 Chapter Eight - Common Investment Abuses By FPA member Tim Sobolewski, CFP®, The Financial Planning Center, Amherst, NY and Joanne Schultz, Esq., of Williamsville NY. Extracted from the Internet November 9, 2015 @ http://www.plannersearch.org/life-events/financial-planning/investments/Common%20Investme nt%20Abuses

Chapter Nine

Frequently Asked Questions (Mutual Funds)

1. Are Mutual Funds Considered Cash Equivalents?

2. Are Mutual Funds Considered Equity Securities?

3. Can Mutual Funds Invest In Derivatives?

4. Can Mutual Funds Invest In Private Equity?

5. Do Mutual Fund Companies Pay Taxes?

6. How Can I Find Tax-Exempt Mutual Funds?

7. How Do Mutual Funds Split

8. How Often Do Mutual Funds Pay Capital Gains

9. How Often Do Mutual Funds Report Their Holdings?

10. Why Do Financial Advisors Have a Fiduciary Responsibility?

11. What is considered a good turnover ratio for a mutual fund?

12. What does a low information ratio tell an investor about a mutual fund?

13. What Does a High Information Ratio Tell an Investor About a Mutual Fund?

14. In What Ways Are ETFs More Tax Efficient Than Mutual Funds?

15. In what situations would mutual fund fees be higher than ETF fees?

16. How Do You Calculate The Excess Return of an ETF or Indexed Mutual Fund?

17. How can I use fundamental analysis techniques to evaluate a mutual fund?

18. How can I calculate the tracking error of an ETF or indexed mutual fund?

19. How can a mutual fund raise or lower its turnover ratio?

20. How are a mutual fund's C shares different from A and B shares?

21. Do mutual funds invest only in stocks?

22. Why are mutual funds not FDIC-insured?

23.   Can mutual funds invest in commodities?

24. Can mutual funds invest in IPOs?

25. Can mutual funds outperform savings accounts?

26. Can mutual funds invest in private companies?

27. Does index trading increase market vulnerability?

28. What is the difference between passive and active asset management?

1. Are Mutual Funds Considered Cash Equivalents?

While mutual funds are generally regarded as liquid assets, not all of them are viewed as cash equivalents.

Cash equivalents are simply defined as investment securities that are temporary and which are highly liquid as well as have high credit quality. A highly liquid security is one which can be easily sold or purchased on short notice without any noticeable change in its cost. Assets that are considered illiquid include real estate as selling them on short notice would force the seller to do so at a lower price compared to the current market rates. The maturity period of cash equivalents is three months or less but despite that, they are relatively stable. Moreover, cash equivalents carry a very low risk of change in value.

Types of mutual funds

Generally, there are four main types of mutual funds and they include money market, balance, bond and stock. Just as the names imply, bond and stock funds simply consist of investments in the bonds and stock markets respectively. Stock funds are flexible in that they can be customized to suit a variety of investment goals ranging from a diversified portfolio whose objective is to minimize loss to a high risk but high rewarding strategy. Bond funds are stable and produce slow, steady income with time. Balance funds are a combination of both stock funds and bond funds and they provide a medium amount of risk. Money markets, also known as cash equivalents, are composed of short-term securities that are likely to mature within a period of three months or less.

The advantages and disadvantages of money market funds

Despite the fact that they carry a lower risk compared to corporate debt issues and stocks, there are a number of positives and negatives that investors should be aware of when it comes to money market funds. The positives include;

- Lower risk which makes them a great place to park money
- They generally trade in securities that in high demand including T-bills and as such, they are more liquid. This makes it possible for investors to purchase and sell them with ease.

The negatives of money market funds include;

- The purchasing power may suffer particularly if the inflation is at a higher percentage compared to the rate at which the fund generates returns
- Expenses can take a toll making it hard for investors to keep up with inflation
- Returns may vary especially since they may be required to take higher risks to generate profits for investors

2. Are Mutual Funds Considered Equity Securities?

An equity security can be defined as any investment vehicle where one or more of the investors are part owner of the controlling company. If a company has a total of 100 shares and an investor purchases ten of them, then he/she owns ten percent and he/she is entitle to 10% of the net profits of the controlling company in the event of liquidation.

Ordinary shares that are purchased and traded on a daily basis in the stock market are the frequently transacted equity securities. Investing in equity securities grants an investor the right to take part in various aspects of running the company as well as the possibility to generate income regularly in the form of dividends. Therefore if an investor buys shares from a given company's stock, they own a small proportion of the controlling company.

A mutual fund refers to an investment vehicle that consists of resources pooled by several investors with the main aim of investing them in securities that range from money market instruments and bonds to stocks and similar assets. Money managers are often put in charge of mutual funds and they are responsible for investing the fund's capital to generate capital gains for the investors. A mutual fund's portfolio is structured in such a way that it matches the financial objectives and goals outlined in the prospectus.

The difference between buying a car dealership with ten of your closest friends and selling your car to make a few bucks is more or less the same as the difference between putting your money in mutual funds and putting in stocks. Buying and selling your own is beneficial in that you get all the profit. However, the returns may not be that good if you can't afford a high-end car. On the other hand, buying a car dealership with your friends will allow you to leverage the funds to generate more profits. And while you may have to split the proceeds, the collective investment funds can be used to sell a wider variety of products and/or services. In the same manner, mutual funds pool resources from a number of investors and invest them in bonds, stocks and other highly liquid assets.

So are mutual funds regarded as equity securities? The short answer is yes. Mutual funds are regarded as equity securities since investors buy shares that relate to a proprietorship prize in the fund as a whole.

3. Can Mutual Funds Invest In Derivatives?

The simple answer is yes. Mutual funds can invest up to fifty percent of all net assets in derivatives. Unlike other investment options, the mutual funds industry of the United States is different. For starters, this industry operates under the Investment Company Act of 1940, which dates back to several decades before the existence of derivative markets. As such, the regulations of using mutual funds to invest in derivatives are not up to date or designed to handle the current market. Regardless of this setback, there is a way to ensure that mutual funds are conservative and generate good returns.

But really, what are derivatives? Put in simple terms, these are financial instruments that are based on contracts on agreements and whose values are tied to assets, indexes or instruments. Examples of derivatives include credit default swaps, interest rate swaps, and options on future contracts, forward currency contracts and futures.

While they might include derivatives in their portfolios, mutual funds are generally safe to invest in. to check what percentage of a mutual funds' net assets are tied up in derivatives, one can check the mutual funds' prospectus. Publicly available SEC filings and forms or the company's website can provide the relevant information you require if reviewed well. A Fidelity representative is also a good source of information regarding a mutual fund and how it is invested. If the mutual fund has more than fifty percent of the net assets invested in derivatives, you should take time to consider your options before investing in the mutual fund. The great news about derivatives can greatly boost the returns. The only disadvantage of derivatives is that they are subject to market risk, management risk, credit risk as well as liquidity and interest rate risk.

It is important for investors to understand that the mutual fund's derivative strategy will be successful. A sophisticated risk management process can help investors to identify and manage derivative exposures within a mutual fund. Investors should consider their financial circumstances and risk tolerance level before investing mutual funds in derivatives. Some mutual funds can use derivatives as a core strategy or a short term investment technique.

In addition to mutual funds, derivatives can be used for other purposes including obtaining exposure to an area that's not possible to invest in directly, making speculative investments on the movement of the value of an underlying asset and creating optionability where the value of derivatives is linked to a specific event or condition. In general, derivatives create leverage and as such, a small movement in the value of an underlying asset can result in great returns.

4. Can Mutual Funds Invest In Private Equity?

While investing in private companies can have really good returns, they can also expose investors to greater risks of not being able to dispose of their investments when market conditions become unfavorable. This shortcoming is referred to as illiquidity. To avoid such an issue, mutual funds invest resources by buying other investment companies that specialize in investing into private securities and debts as well as managing their own private investments.

For instance, Red Rocks Listed Private Equity Fund specializes in investing into other highly reputable private companies such as the

Blackstone Group, Eurazeo, Aurelius, the Carlyle Group, and HarbourVest Global Private Equity. Since the Red Rocks Listed Private Equity Fund does not invest directly into private equity, it adds another layer of fees and management that investors have to pay for.

Due to SEC's rules and regulations regarding illiquid security holdings, mutual funds have to exercise a certain degree of restrictions when it comes to purchasing private equity directly. For starters, SEC guidelines only allow up to fifteen percent to illiquid securities. In addition, mutual funds have their own regulations that govern investment in illiquid equity and debt securities. As such, mutual funds that invest in private equity are those of the fund of funds type.

Why are mutual funds making private equity investments as part of their strategy? For starters, private investments are likely to offer higher returns because the level of risk involved is high. Secondly, private companies are generally difficult to trade or even value. Shares offered by public companies in private can be purchased at a discount to the regular stock price. Finally, the Securities and Exchange Commission has put in restrictions on how much mutual funds can invest in illiquid securities.

Private equities can only make up a small percentage of a fund's portfolio. The SEC puts a restriction of a maximum of 15% that a mutual fund's total assets that can be invested in securities that can be traded thinly or illiquid. Mutual funds place lower restrictions on investing in private equity while most funds don't invest in them at all.

So can mutual funds invest in private equities? Absolutely. They can do so by buying shares of publicly listed private equities indirectly. Mutual funds that do so are generally referred to as fund of funds. Making direct investments in private equity is impossible due to restrictions put in place by the Securities and Exchange Commission.

5. Do Mutual Fund Companies Pay Taxes?

Taxes are a key consideration for investors, particularly mutual fund shareholders. Generally, mutual fund shareholders are required to pay federal, local and even state taxes, including taxes on dividends and capital gains. Those who own mutual funds outside of tax-advantaged are taxed annually on the sale of fund shares as well as distributions from the fund.

Interest that is generated from municipal bonds is generally exempt from federal taxes and in special cases, local and state taxes too. If mutual funds distribute income generated in the same way to shareholders, the distributions are also exempt from tax. Even though income generated from such funds is generally exempted from tax, it still has to be reported.

In the event that a shareholder sells their mutual fund shares, he/she will experience either a loss or gain in the year that the shares are sold. In such a case, the shareholder would be liable for tax on any capital gains just as they would be if they sold individual securities.

A mutual fund holds several financial securities with the sole purpose of earning investment dividends, income, interest and capital gains. However, since a mutual fund is a regulated investment company under Regulation M of the Internal Revenue Service, it is required to distribute income to its clients who are then taxed individually at their personal taxation rates. This procedure ensures that double taxation on mutual funds and investors does not occur.

So do mutual fund companies pay taxes? Generally, mutual funds don't have to pay taxes if they meet certain regulatory requirements. They are incorporated as regulated investment companies under the Internal Revenue Code and as such, they are generally exempt from taxes given the fact that their earnings are passed in form of distributions to the investors. A mutual fund is similar to a limited partnership in that it represents an investment vehicle that pools resources from investors. The earnings are ultimately distributed to shareholders who are taxed at their individual taxation rates.

As an investment company, certain requirements have to be met a mutual fund in order to enjoy its conduit status and be exempt from tax. For starters, at least ninety percent of a mutual fund's earnings should originate from the investment income like interest, dividend and capital gains income. Moreover, the fund has to distribute at least 90% of its earnings in order to maintain the regulated investment company status. If less than 98% of the net income is distributed, an excise tax of 4% is imposed by the IRC.

6. How Can I Find Tax-Exempt Mutual Funds?

Tax-exempt mutual funds can easily be found at prominent investment companies. Many mutual funds offer a wide range of investment options to ensure that all investors are taken care of. Put simply, tax-exempt mutual funds consist of investments whose returns are tax-free.

What's a mutual fund?

It is a type of investment that's highly liquid security popular among investors. While mutual fund is classified as an investment type of company, the term is also used to refer to the fund's portfolio. In the case of mutual funds, investors pool their resources together to leverage their collective investing power. They purchase shares of the mutual fund - the same way as buying stock shares – and this entitles each of them a certain percentage of the proceeds. A mutual fund invests the contributions of the shareholders into a variety of securities that may include bonds, short-term debts and stocks. The profits are distributed among the shareholders according to their ownership stakes.

Types of mutual funds

Generally, there are four main types of mutual funds and they include money market, balance, bond and stock. Just as the names imply, bond and stock funds simply consist of investments in the bonds and stock markets respectively. Stock funds are flexible in that they can be customized to suit a variety of investment goals ranging from a diversified portfolio whose objective is to minimize loss to a high risk but high rewarding strategy. Bond funds are stable and produce slow, steady income with time. Balance funds are a combination of both stock funds and bond funds and they provide a medium amount of risk. Money markets, also known as cash equivalents, are composed of short-term securities that are likely to mature within a period of three months.

Tax-exempt funds

Mutual funds that are invested in municipal or government bonds are known as tax-exempt funds. They are named so because the interest generated by such investments is not subject to tax. In some cases, interest generated by bonds in your state of residency may be exempt from state, local and federal taxes. Interest on some bonds may still be subject to federal tax even if it is exempt from local and/or state tax. This includes interest generated from Treasury bonds.

Due to the fact that they consist of government-issued bonds, tax-exempt mutual funds generally generate lower rate of returns compared to volatile funds. In some cases, the tax benefits of these types of investments outweigh the reduction in the earning potential.

7. How Do Mutual Funds Split?

Mutual funds split more or less like individual stocks splits with less frequency. The only economic effect of mutual fund split is that they don't have any effect on the net value of the fund and as such, they are used purely as a marketing strategy.

What is a mutual fund split?

A split occurs when the number of outstanding shares of a mutual fund is increased while at the same time reducing the unit price of shares by the same factor. The Net Asset Value (NAV) per share refers to the price of a mutual fund share. The NAV represents the total value of a fund's portfolio, minus all liabilities, dividend by the number of outstanding shares.

Compared to individual stocks, splits are less common in mutual funds. The most common splits include 3:1 and 2:1. A 3:1 split occurs when the number of shares is tripled while the price of individual shares is reduced by one third of the original value. On the other hand, a 2:1 split occurs when the number of shares is doubled while the price of individual shares is reduced by half of the original value.

If a mutual fund splits its shares, the total value of any investor's investment is not affected. However, the price for new shareholders as well as ownership stake represented by each share goes down. Assuming you own 100 shares with a mutual fund whose Net Asset Value is $500, if the mutual fund announces a 2:1 split, you will own 200 shares whose NAV per share is $250.

Why mutual funds split

Like split stocks, the main objective of splitting a mutual fund is to attract more investors. But since splits don't affect any gains generated in future, their effect is entirely psychological. If the prices of shares become too high, thinking that they are priced out of the market is the common reaction among prospective investors. A split results in a lower price per share and as such, investors might think that they are within their range. This encourages them to invest in the fund. The fortunate or unfortunate truth is that whether or not a mutual fund is split, an investment in the fund has the same value. In the scenario discussed in the previous paragraph, $100,000 would have purchased 20 shares before the split and 40 shares after the split. However, the value of the investment would still be $10,000 in both cases.

8. How Often Do Mutual Funds Pay Capital Gains

The frequency with which mutual funds pay capital gains varies. However, mutual funds that generate profits within a particular financial year are required to pay capital gains to all the shareholders at least once or twice every year. These distributions are made primarily for tax reasons. Once paid, investors can choose to reinvest their gains or take them as cash. Many investors choose to reinvest their gains and this increases the shares in their account.

Defining mutual funds

Mutual funds simply refer to investment firms that pool collective investment of thousands of shareholders and invest it into a variety of bonds and stocks among other financial securities. Every shareholder is entitled to a percentage of the fund's profits and may receive dividend distributions and capital gains several times throughout the year. Mutual funds are customizable and highly liquid, thus a popular investment option for many people.

Defining capital gain

If an investor sells a capital asset, say a bond or a stock, for more than the purchase cost, the investor makes a profit which in this case is known as a capital gain. For instance, if a bond was purchased at a cost of $150 but sold for $200, the capital gain in this case is $50. If a mutual fund sells a security at a profit, such a sale also generates capital gain.

There are two types of capital gains; long-term and short-term. The latter are distributed to shareholders as income dividends and are also subject to ordinary income taxes. On the other hand, long-term capital gains are subject to a maximum tax rate of 20% which is not inclusive of 3.8% surtax that's applicable to net investment income for higher income taxpayers.

While dividends and capital gains both represent a source of investment income for shareholders, mutual funds dividends and capital gains shouldn't be confused. Capital gains are only generated when mutual funds are sold while dividends are generated only when a portfolio asset pays interest or dividends. The most common sources of dividends are coupon-bearing bonds and dividend paying stocks.

What are the tax implications of capital gains?

The frequency of dividend distributions and capital gains is important. And while a profit on an investment is a good thing, it comes with a tax burden. Any income that is received from mutual funds should be included in an investor's taxable income. However, gains from investments held by the mutual funds for more than a year are taxed at a lower rate compared to the ordinary income. Your tax bill may skyrocket if your funds generate capital gains often.

9. How Often Do Mutual Funds Report Their Holdings?

Technically known as an open-end company, mutual funds raise money by selling their own shares to investors. The money collected is used to buy a portfolio of short-term money market instruments, bonds, stocks, others shares or securities, or a combination of the above. Every share is a representation of ownership slice of the mutual fund. The proportional right of an investor depends entirely on the number of shares that he/she owns as well as the capital gains and profits generated from its investments. Investments made by a mutual fund depend on the financial objectives of the investors as well as the skills and management styles of the funds' professional managers. The holdings of a mutual fund constitute its underlying investments and their performance determines the investment return of the fund.

Mutual funds are obliged by the Securities and Exchange Commission to report their holdings at the end of every quarter because they are regulated investment companies. At the end if every fiscal quarter, mutual funds use SEC Forms N-CSR and N-Q to report their quarterly holdings. Both of the above forms are available on SEC's websites. In addition to filling the forms, companies are obliged to reveal their holdings on their official websites.

Mutual funds disclosures timings

Reports regarding mutual funds' holdings are available to the public through the SEC's Edgar online database. Mutual funds are required to file their holdings with the SEC within 60 days after the end of a fiscal quarter. Not many mutual funds adhere to this condition and as such, they end up reporting their holdings in an untimely manner. On the other hand, some holdings choose to report their holdings more frequently, with some reporting them every month, but this is not a common practice because it requires more effort and additional cost.

Mutual funds required disclosures

SEC regulation requires mutual funds to provide full disclosures of their portfolio schedules on a quarterly basis. The filings must be certified by the funds' financial officers and principal executive. While management analysis and discussion is not really a mandatory requirement, some managers comment on their mutual funds' performance every quarter.

The main importance of quarterly reports to investors is that they help them assess whether and how mutual funds are complying with their investment goals. SEC is yet to review a proposal that suggested monthly holdings report requirement for registered investment companies including mutual funds. The timely disclosure of holdings can help investors monitor funds closely and make informed investment decisions. Due to this, some investors may attach substantial value to more frequent holdings disclosure.

10. Why Do Financial Advisors Have a Fiduciary Responsibility?

Financial advisors are governed by Fiduciary law which requires them to act in the best interest of their clients all the time. This importance of this is that it protects investors from advisors who may want to take advantage.

Defining fiduciary duty

Fiduciary duty is considered one of the highest legal obligations. By law, a fiduciary is always required to act in the interests of his client, who is otherwise known as the principal. Fiduciary duty applies to a variety of professionals including corporate directors and attorneys. They both have fiduciary duty to their shareholders and clients respectively.

Fiduciary duty also requires fiduciaries to avoid conflict of interest that may result in them providing sub-standard service to their clients, the principals. Put simply, this calls for avoiding scenarios where the personal interests of a fiduciary clash with those of the principal. For instance, a lawyer is not allowed to represent a client who is suing the firm where the lawyer's fiancée works.

Fiduciary duty in the world of finance

Fiduciary duty in investment and finance is especially important since there are several ways in which an advisor can gain at the expense of their clients' interests. Despite the emphasis on its importance, not all financial advisors are subject to the constraints of fiduciary duty. This includes any advisors who aren't registered with the Securities and Exchange Commission and similar state security regulators. This type of registration is not mandatory for financial advisors, and they are only bound by a suitability standard that requires them to make recommendations about investments suitable for their principals' financial goals.

Discerning among financial advisors

Technically, the aim of most financial advisors today is not to rip off clients.

However, it is also challenging for investors to know which type of financial advisors are held to which standard i.e. fiduciary or suitability. The compensation plan for advisors who are held accountable by the suitability standard is likely to lead to conflict of interest even though media advertisement may suggest otherwise.

Increasing investor education would go a long way in reducing the information gap that exists between principals and financial advisors. While in many cases they know very little about the products they are sold, they should at least know what type of advisor they are working with. One of the easiest ways to know the accountability standard of your advisor is to ask if they are acting under the fiduciary standard and if they can put that in writing.

11. What is considered a good turnover ratio for a mutual fund?

It is important to note from the onset that having high or low turnover ratio in a mutual fund is never a clear indicator of how the fund performs. When the ratio is high it does not directly translate to higher profit nor does a low ratio indicate reduced earnings over the reporting period. Therefore, the question of what a good turnover ratio is for a mutual fund is best answered when considering the various factors that are involved in a mutual fund. These factors range from the fund's composition and structure, the specified investment objectives over the short and long term, and the specific strategy that the fund management will employ in the execution of trades. When determining a reasonably proper turnover ratio for a selected fund, one has to go beyond the consideration of the above-listed parameters. It will be helpful to obtain the best estimate through conducting comparisons of turnover ratios of mutual funds that are similar to the one being assessed. Further comparisons should be done with the mutual fund's current turnover ratio in relation to the performance in the previous reporting periods.

Calculating the turnover ratio

In mutual funds, the turnover ratio signifies the amount of total equity of a fund that has been sold and replenished with a different portfolio, usually over the previous year. The formula for calculating this ratio is a division of the purchases made or sales of part of the fund (the lower value is considered), by the average net assets of the fund in a month. Any securities that have maturity periods lasting less than a year are not considered in the calculation.

Scrutinizing Turnover Ratios

There are different types of mutual funds, and they all offer various types of turnover ratios. The funds include stock, bond, index and funds that are actively managed. Because of the different management styles and trade execution objectives, some funds will typically report low turnover ratios though they are performing optimally while other funds with aggressive trade executions strategies may have turnover ratios exceeding 100%. However, conscious investors are advised to look for funds that have turnover ratios in the range of 50-70%. When looking for an efficient portfolio management, turnover ratios should not be the only guide to determining the mutual fund to invest, but as one of the elements. More focus should be given to the ability of the fund to be a profitable investment. Therefore, determining the funds that are acceptable to have low turnover ratios and those with high ratios will be crucial in guiding decision making in this area.

12. What does a low information ratio tell an investor about a mutual fund?

The information ratio refers to a ratio that measures a portfolio's returns as compared to the benchmark returns, which are normally an index, to the volatile nature of the returns. The ratio is a measure of how capable a manager is in the generation of returns that are more than the set benchmark and also can determine how consistent an investor is. The ratio is indicative of whether the manager surpassed the benchmark and to what extent in the particular period of evaluation. When the information ratio is high, it is indicative that the manager is more consistent, and consistency is a good trait to have. The ratio is calculated by using the formula below;

$$\text{Information Ratio} = \frac{(R_p - R_i)}{S_{p\text{-}i}}$$

Where:

Rp = represents returns made from the portfolio

Ri = represents returns on the index or benchmark

Sp-i = is the standard deviation or margin of error that is allowed for the difference between the Rp and Ri.

The ratio is in essence used to measure how the manager of a mutual fund that is active is performing. By using the information ratios, an investor can be able to tell if the manager can outperform the benchmark and by what margin. The ratio also indicates the period that the manager can take or sustain the outperformance on the benchmark. When the ratio is low, the indication is that the mutual fund is not optimally performing and should not be considered for investment. On the other hand, a high IR is indicative of the active fund manager being touted to perform most likely beyond the benchmark for a longer period

When the information ratio of a mutual fund is significantly low, it means that the active manager of the fund is incapable of producing results that are going to go beyond the benchmark or has been producing results that are below par for a prolonged period. A very low information ratio means that the manager has not been able to get results that are more than the benchmark for any period. A negative IR means that the mutual fund was not able to produce any amount of excess returns.

Ratios that are less than 0.4 indicate that the mutual fund was not able to produce excess returns for a given period, hence rendering the investment unviable. Ratios ranging between 0.4 and 0.6 render such mutual funds viable investment options with those that get to the 0.6 - 1mark being considered excellent investment opportunities.

13. What Does a High Information Ratio Tell an Investor About a Mutual Fund?

When there is a high information ratio, it is indicative that the manager is more consistent, and consistency is a desirable trait to possess as a manager. The information ratio is a ratio that measures the returns of a portfolio as compared to the benchmark returns, which are normally an index, to the volatile nature of the returns. The ratio is a measure of how capable a manager is in the generation of returns that are more than the set benchmark and also can determine how consistent an investor is. The ratio is indicative of whether the manager surpassed the benchmark and to what extent in the particular period of evaluation. The ratio is calculated by using the formula below;

The abbreviations

$$\text{Information Ratio} = \frac{(R_p - R_i)}{S_{p-i}}$$

mean:

Rp = returns made from the portfolio

Ri = returns on the index or benchmark

Sp-i = standard deviation or margin of error that is allowed for the difference between the Rp and Ri.

A high IR is indicative of the active fund manager being touted to perform most likely beyond the benchmark for a longer period,

On the other hand when the ratio is low; the indication is that the mutual fund is not optimally performing and should not be considered for investment. The ratio is in essence used to measure how the manager of a mutual fund that is active is performing. By using the information ratios, an investor can tell if the manager can outperform the benchmark and by what margin. The ratio also indicates the period that the manager can take or sustain the outperformance on the benchmark.

When the information ratio of a mutual fund is high, it is an indication to investors that the active manager of the fund has done a tremendous job in ensuring that there are high returns and has been doing so consistently for an extended period. Mutual funds that possess high IRs are suitable to be chosen by potential investors. When considering the IRs in making an investment decision, the higher the value of IR, the better investment in the mutual fund is going to become. A zero or below information ratio indicates that manager was unable to produce excess results and investors should avoid investing in the fund. The most common ratios range between 0.4 and 1 and present viable investment opportunities. Ratios above one are quite rare but they are precious if an investor can get one of that sort.

14. In What Ways Are ETFs More Tax Efficient Than Mutual Funds?

Apart from ETFs being less costly in operational costs, they also provide higher tax efficiency when compared to mutual funds. To demonstrate this, it will cost an investor less in tax liabilities if they hold

ETFs in a taxable account as compared to holding structured mutual funds in the same taxable account. How the ETFs and mutual funds are treated by the internal revenue service (IRS) is the same. They are both subjected to capital gains tax, and the income dividend is also taxed. The difference in tax efficiency comes from the manner on which the ETFs are structured. Their structure makes the taxes incurred by the holder of the ETF to be minimized and the overall tax bill to be paid. This is because, after the sale of ETFs, the capital gains tax incurred is less than what another investor in a mutual fund will be required to pay.

What makes ETFs more efficient in taxes is the fact that – according to tax professionals – minor events that can be taxed in the manner in which a normal ETF is structured as compared to a mutual fund. The reasons include:

- As opposed to the operation of ETFs, management of mutual funds has to rebalance continually the fund by re-selling and buying securities so as to cover for the shareholders that redeem their equity and re-allocate assets to the new and or remaining shareholders. The continuous trading within the mutual fund results in capital gains tax for shareholders, the cost is even transferred to shareholders who might not have participated in the in-trading.

- On the other hand, the management of ETFs takes the growth or reduction in investments by redeeming a pool of assets that predict the entirety of the exposure of the ETF investments. The result is that the investors are rarely exposed to capital gains tax on individual securities that they hold within the ETF.

However, some strategies can be employed by the manager of mutual funds to mitigate the high tax burdens that they face. For example, they take advantage of carrying capital losses from prior years to do the tax-loss harvesting. There are also types of mutual funds like the index mutual funds that offer higher tax efficiency than other actively managed funds because of the low turnover that they report. ETFs are preferable because of the transparency that they offer in their operations as compared to mutual funds. However, not all ETFs are efficient. There are international ETFs that are invested in growing markets and are often lesser in efficiency as compared to ETFs in the domestic market.

15. In what situations would mutual fund fees be higher than ETF fees?

Though there are specific situations where mutual fund fees are higher than ETF fees, ETFs are usually less costly. The exceptions call for the examination from the part of investors to determine relative costs of mutual funds and ETFs that track similar indices. Even with such similarities, the ETFs are always better advantaged regarding cost because of the structural difference it bears from mutual funds. Mutual funds have some costs that are transparent and others that are not as transparent, usually not revealed in the cost calculation but add up as additional expenses. The structure of mutual funds makes such costs arise, but there are those that are not necessary to the process and end up being just an extra unnecessary burden to the investor. It is possible to get mutual funds that have costs that are a little cheaper; others even a lot cheaper, but it is almost impossible to get a mutual fund that has no costs at all. ETFs are not sacred cows either; they come with both transparent and hidden fees as well. The difference between them is that they are lesser in number and cost much lower than their counterparts.

For mutual funds, all transactions that take place within and their associated costs are transferred to the shareholders. The charges range from charges for distribution, fees of operations, and costs related to transfer-agent. On top of that, the annual capital gains tax bill is also passed on to the shareholder's equity in the mutual fund. The effect is reduced returns on investments

(ROI) for the shareholders. There is also the situation where many mutual funds charge a sales load depending on the class of shares that a shareholder has in the mutual fund. The sales load is a fee charged by the fund management for allowing an investor the chance to invest with them.

ETFs are basically individual securities whose design is made to track certain indices, baskets of investment assets or commodities. Just like the trading of regular stocks, the ETFs are traded in a similar manner with shares being able to be traded individually on an exchange. Mutual funds are designed in a manner that allows investors to buy and sell them through companies that offer the mutual fund as they cannot be exchange traded. The popularity of ETFs has been on an upward pedestal since their introduction as they are highly liquid, offer easier trading options and are cost efficient.

16. How Do You Calculate The Excess Return of an ETF or Indexed Mutual Fund?

What is excess return? It is also referred to as the 'alpha' or 'the rate of return that is abnormal'. It is the part of a portfolio return or security that is not defined by the market's overall rate of return. Excess returns are common as a result of the skills employed by the investor or manager of a portfolio. It is a measure widely used by investors and analysts in determining risk-adjusted performance. For (ETFs), exchange-traded funds the measure of risk-adjusted is supposed to be similar to the excess return. This is the measure that normally exceeds the benchmark of the instrument or in the case of mutual funds, the annual expense ratio. Getting the value of indexed mutual funds is the easiest of all when pitted against the benchmark. It is just a subtraction of the total returns of the benchmark from the net assets of the fund to get the excess return. As a result of the many expenses incurred by a mutual fund, the excess return is mostly negative for all index funds.

As a norm, keen investors are always interested in mutual funds and ETFs that perform beyond the benchmarks they are pitted against and consistently produce positive excess returns. However, it is important to recognize the difficulty that is associated with consistently being able to produce excess returns in mutual funds that are managed. This is because of the high fees related to such funds and the ever-changing market dynamics.

Formula

To better illustrate the calculation of excess returns; take an example of a fund portfolio manager that expects the returns of the fund to be 15% the following year. The year ends and the actual returns are at 16%. The excess return is value by which the fund's returns exceeded the benchmark, which is 1%. In mathematical terms, the excess returns are the rates of returns that exceed what was aimed at initially. This measure is a definite way of determining if the skills that a manager possesses are adding value to the fund's portfolio on a risk-adjusted basis.

Some skeptics believe in the hypothesis of the efficient market. Hence, they discredit the idea that a manager's skills can result in consistent excess returns. They think it is a matter of chance and that there is not a significant difference in the returns that active portfolio managers and those that apply passive investment strategies can make for their clients.

17. How can I use fundamental analysis techniques to evaluate a mutual fund?

When investing, fundamental analysis is the pillar upon which investments are based. For one to be considered doing solid investments, fundamental analysis is a must. However, the subject of fundamental analysis is quite broad and can be confusing for starters on where to begin. Despite the fact different strategies can be used to make investments, they all use fundamentals. Fundamental analysis is widely involved with a critical look at the statements of finances. It is also referred to as quantitative analysis. It is involved with looking at the assets, revenues, expenses, credit owed among other determinant financial aspects of a company.

In evaluating a mutual fund, there is more than just understanding what the numbers mean. It is also a part qualitative analysis where the often difficult-to-measure intangible aspects of the company are assessed. At its core, fundamental analysis is concerned with the understanding of the risks associated with a mutual fund and determining the fund that is managed in a prudent manner. As a fundamental analyst, some key techniques are to look at the stocks held by the fund and their performance, check the statement of finances and review the mode of governance that is used in the management of the portfolio. In the area of mutual funds, the techniques that will guide the evaluation of the fund include looking at the bond and stock strategies being used by the management, concentration and sector match-ups among other elements that are critical to the construction and management of a mutual fund's portfolio.

As an investor, a keen eye should be necessary so as to enable looking beyond the impressive performance of a mutual fund in the past and question whether that trend is likely to continue into the future. For example, a company where the mutual fund has shares might have done some revolutionary thing that consumers loved. However, over time, there are going to be an imitator and the competition in the market is going to drive the profitability of such shares downwards. The trick here is to look for mutual funds that are in a line of business that makes it hard for others to imitate.

Metrics to consider in Fundamental Mutual Fund analysis

When making decisions to invest, or not, the following are among the reasons a fundamental analyst should look at:

- The consistency of the company in making profits and the future outlook
- How the company is performing relative to the competitors in the market.
- Is the company able to meet its obligations to creditors in an adequate manner?

18. How can I calculate the tracking error of an ETF or indexed mutual fund?

It is necessary to first understand what a tracking error is. A tracking error for index mutual funds or ETF is a measurement of the returns that arise as a result of the net asset value of the fund in relation to the returns made by the index over a period. In a real life calculation, if a particular index gains 3% over one year, while the fund that is used to track it improves by 2.7%, the tracking error will be the difference, in this case, 0.3% points for the period under review.

For most of the conventional mutual funds, the calculations of tracking errors are done in a straightforward manner. These conventional mutual funds are those that are traded once daily basing on their net asset value (NAV). The tracking error is calculated at the end of the day based on the per-share value of the holdings of the fund. This is the similar methodology that is applied to the exchanged-traded funds despite the fact ETF shares are easily traded throughout the day at prices that hover around the NAV. Investors are advised to be knowledgeable of the fact that premiums whose value is below or above that of the net asset value are not reflected when making calculations of the tracking error, although they are important in making returns considerations.

The formula for calculating the tracking error is subtracting the cumulative returns of the benchmark from the returns of the portfolio as shown below:

$Return_p - Return_i = Tracking\ Error$

Where:

p = portfolio

i = index or benchmark

The measurement of a tracking error for either a mutual fund or ETF can be done several times, but it is more significant in meaning when considerations of the trends it delivers are observed. Some factors are key in determining the tracking error that a portfolio will present. They include:

- The extent to which the benchmark and the portfolio's securities are common

- Factors important in both the benchmark and portfolio like the timing of investments, management style applied among other fundamental characteristics.

- The weighing differences of the NAV of the portfolio and benchmark

- How volatile the benchmark is and the beta of the portfolio

Most index funds do not perform in the same manner, nor do they all meet the expected index or benchmark that they were made to track. It is recommended by analysts to consider the tracking error as a guiding factor in choosing one index fund over the other.

19. How can a mutual fund raise or lower its turnover ratio?

A mutual fund can achieve an effect of increased or decreased turnover ratio depending on how the fund manager operates it. The manager can, through changes in trading activities through a year's period, raise or lower the turnover ratio. The turnover ratio is often used by investors and analysts to gauge the activities and obligations that a fund management is undertaking. The ratio specifically looks at the total sales achieved by the fund against its assets. The ratio is an indicator of the number of times that each invested dollar is sold, and the proceeds reinvested to grow the asset base in a given period.

Active fund managers are known to make several trades throughout the year. It is a management style known to bear significant risks to the investors, but also results in great chances for making profits if the trades bear fruit. The fund manager that knows how to take calculated risks often is suitable for investors that have the guts to take big risks in return for increased chances of making handsome profits. However, investors that are not into taking risks frequently are better off dealing with a fund manager that makes few trades through the period of a year.

What is the Turnover Ratio?

This is a ratio that is also known as the investment rate of turnover. It is achieved by calculating the total assets of the fund divided by total sales made by the fund over a selected period, usually one year. An example is if a fund has $2 million in total sales and $6 million in total assets. The turnover ratio will be 0.3, or 30%. This has the implication that the total value of the fund's equity worth 30% is exchanged in the form of trades on an annual basis. When the turnover ratio exceeds or reaches 100%, it implies that the fund's portfolio has been changed in totality over the period in question.

When the ratios are high, it means that the management of the fund is active while low ratios imply that the management takes a rather passive administration style. When as a fund manager you employ the strategy of buying and holding, the turnover ratio will most likely be low as the style requires very few trades are conducted once the fund has been invested in fully. Investors and analysts pay close attention to the trends of turnover ratios before selecting a fund manager. This is because as indicated, the style of management employed determines the turnover ratios recorded.

20. How are a mutual fund's C shares different from A and B shares?

While there exist different types of mutual funds, it is possible to have a single mutual fund that has a unitary portfolio and a sole advisor on investments, but different classes of shares. The different classes represent interests that are similar to the portfolio of the mutual fund. The main difference is the cost the mutual fund charges investors regarding fees and expenses depending on the class selected. When a product is charged a high price, it is most likely to be of quality. This same mantra is not applicable in matters that deal with investment in mutual funds.

It has never been proven that investors pay higher fees to get better returns on their investments. The manager of such a high-cost fund might make riskier investments decisions in the hope of generating higher returns and end up making losses. Instead of increasing the portfolio of investors through the huge amounts they paid, the results become the inverse with capital losses leading to shrinking value of the portfolio.

Investors are advised to be keen in selecting the class of shares in a mutual fund so as to evade paying exorbitant fees that are not a guarantee of making profits out of their investments.

Class C shares are among the main three types of mutual fund shares that exist. The others are Class A and Class B shares. The differences between the three categories of shares are their unique structures and load fees associated with each. Among the many differences, class C shares are easily distinguishable from the others as they are level-load shares. The meaning of this is that the money paid to the mutual fund is invested in shares in totality. Unlike the others that charge a percentage of the initial investment as commission, class C shareholders are allowed to pay commissions the mutual fund on an annual basis.

Class A shares, on the other hand, have a charge called the front-end load. This means that when money is invested in the buying of this class of shares, a certain percentage of that initial investment is subtracted to act as fees and commissions. In this scenario, the total amount of money invested is not all directed to the purchase of shares as a certain amount is taken out for commissions and fees. Just like class C shares, Class B shares also invest the whole sum of money towards buying shares. However, these shares have a back-end load charge. The charges are subtracted when an investor is selling the shares by taking a percentage of the gains made.

21. Do mutual funds invest only in stocks?

Mutual funds do not only invest in stocks, there are certain types that invest in corporate bonds and government bonds as well. When investing in stocks, the value will depend on the changes in the market, therefore they offer a potentially much higher return compared to bonds. But on the other hand the risk is also higher, when the market is going to an undesirable direction, it will result in a great loss.

While bonds are much less risky than stocks, but they provide a fixed return that's usually lower than stocks. The only potential loss from a bond security is when an extraordinary situation appears, like a total failure of a corporation that will prevent it from giving the return to the investors.

Bonds can be sub classified based on the types and maturity of the bonds. Types of bonds include municipal bonds, government bonds, investment-grade corporate bonds, and high-yield/junk bonds. While based on maturity bonds could be sub classified as long-term, intermediate-term and short-term bonds.

The investment profile of mutual funds will be based on the type of funds:

Equity Funds

These mutual funds only invest in common stock. Equity funds provide the highest returns but they are also very risky. However, when compared with individual stocks, the risk of equity funds is still relatively low. That's because equity is actually hundreds or thousands of stocks in a bundle, so when one company included in the bundle is failing, the negative impact to the investor is minimum because the investment is spread across hundreds or even thousands of companies in the bundle.

Fixed Income Funds

These mutual funds only invest in corporate or government bonds that provide fixed returns. Investors will get the same returns whether in a bear market or bull market, so they are less risky. However, just like other types of investments that come with a lower risk, fixed income funds also offer lower returns, at least in most cases.

Balanced Funds

A combination of fixed income and equity investments. The levels of risk and return potentials of balanced funds are somewhere between that of fixed income funds and equity funds. Balanced funds have a large scope, some of them are stock-heavy, while others consist of bonds with a small group of equities. You can find a lot of balanced funds that you can choose nowadays, you can always find the one that suits your personal goals based on your desired return potential and risk tolerance.

Balanced funds provide more diversification compared to buying bonds and stocks individually. In a single balanced fund, an investor could hold hundreds or thousands of stocks and bonds. The great thing is the investor never has to rebalance the balanced fund, because it's done automatically. Some balanced funds maintain a mixed asset, while others grow conservatively over time. The bond portion of the balanced fund will help to counterbalance the risks that occur in the stock portion, therefore the investor will have a "balanced investment.

22. Why are mutual funds not FDIC-insured?

Investment products like Treasury securities, life insurance policies, annuities, stock and bond investments are usually not insured by the FDIC, including mutual funds. People sometimes got confused about it when it comes to money market mutual funds, this is because it's a common knowledge that money market deposit accounts are insured by the FDIC.

Money market mutual funds are very different with money market deposit accounts in terms of risk levels. Even though the risk is actually quite low, but still it's possible for you to lose your original investment in a money market mutual fund. On the other hand, money market deposit accounts carry no risk at all to your funds.

Another common confusion is when it comes to Individual retirement accounts (IRAs). This is because some types of IRA savings investments are FDIC-insured and some not.

Just like the above, the main difference is in the risk levels of these investments. When invested in a money market deposit account or standard savings account, the funds will be insured by the FDIC, but when invested in mutual funds or stocks, the funds will not be insured.

The Federal Deposit Insurance Corporation (FDIC) was created by the US Congress to make sure no one is harmed financially in a devastating financial crisis. During the Great Depression, the banks did not have enough cash for depositors who wanted to withdraw their deposits. Millions of innocent people were losing their life savings in this catastrophic financial disaster. In order to protect the people, the US Congress and the government formed the FDIC. So what you need to understand here is that FDIC was created to protect innocent people from losing money through no fault of their own.

That's why mutual funds and other securities are not insured. That's because these investments carry some risks no matter how small it might be. Investors are using these investment products to make profits, and they also know these investment products come with certain levels of risk and there is a chance they could lose everything. This is why investment products are not insured by the FDIC.

To put it simply, investing actually pretty much like gambling. You put your money on something with a chance of gaining a huge profit or losing everything. When you finally get your profit, that's good for you, but when you lose everything, the only one responsible is yourself because you knew the risk.

However, it doesn't mean that nothing can protect your mutual fund investments. Even though nothing can protect your investment from any loss caused by fluctuations in the market, there is a protection for investors from investment losses due to brokerage firm's failure. You can get this kind of protection from the Securities Investor Protection Corporation (SPIC). This corporation provides protections for mutual fund investments, CDs, Treasury securities, options, and bonds. The SPIC can insure up to $500,000 with a cash sublimit of $250,000.

It's always best to make sure that you choose a safe mutual investment to reduce your risk.

23. Can mutual funds invest in commodities?

Absolutely! In fact, mutual funds even offer a greater chance for investors to gain more exposure to commodities when compared with other exchange traded funds. Commodities are basic goods that are interchangeable with other goods of the same type. These are the type of goods that are often used as 'inputs' to produce other goods or services. Although perhaps there might be a slight difference in the quality of each good, basically they are considered the same by producers. However, it doesn't mean that there is no quality control, when traded on an exchange, these commodities must meet the basis grade, which is the specified minimum standards for commodities to be used as the actual of a futures contract.

There are so many different types of commodities that can be used in trading, as long as there is only little differentiation between the same commodities from different producers. Like oil for example, a barrel of oil coming from different producers is basically the same product. Unlike products such as electronics, where you will find a huge difference between two products from two different producers. Some examples of commodities are grains, beef, soybeans, livestock, wheat and other agricultural products, precious metals like gold and silver, also natural resources like natural gas and oil. Today, the commodity types have expanded to include financial products like foreign currencies and indexes. There are also new types of commodities as a result of technological advances, including cell phone minutes and bandwidth.

There are some great benefits for investing in commodities. Some commodities have lower correlation to the stock market and are considered as a hedge against inflation. Commodities are also great to diversify the holdings in your portfolio.

Commodities trading commonly executed through futures contracts on exchanges with standardized quantity and quality. For instance, a board of trade can specify that one wheat contract is for 5,000 bushels of

No.2 Northern Spring wheat. That means any wheat commodity with less amount and grade cannot be traded.

However, futures contracts require high levels of leverage that will magnify the potential profits and losses. Therefore, mutual funds actually provide a safer way to invest in commodities, because they can minimize the risk of losing too much on commodity investments.

There are many different types of mutual funds that invest in commodities, but generally there are two kinds of commodity mutual funds, those that are actively managed and the others that are passively managed.

Actively managed commodity mutual funds are involving a manager that will actively make investment decisions with the main objective of beating a benchmark index. So the final results will pretty much depend on the manager's skill whether the fund is able to beat the market. Most of the times, this type of commodity mutual funds also have higher expense ratios. Passively managed commodity mutual funds on the other hand, do not aim to outperform the market, instead they only seek to track a benchmark index, that's why this type of commodity mutual funds have lower expense ratios.

24. Can mutual funds invest in IPOs?

It is possible for mutual funds to invest in IPOs, but there are some rules to follow. For examples, most mutual funds usually have bylaws that forbid them to invest in IPOs until the stock has been traded for over six months. The reason is because in many newly issued stocks there seems to be a lack of liquidity that distorts pricing. Another reason is because usually the first six months are mostly dominated by insiders who use market liquidity for unloading their shares and gains in the stock driven by hype instead of fundamentals.

There is a lot of considerations need to be made when investing in IPOs, because many of them are companies with unproven track records and business models. On the other hand, most mutual funds are conservative and they only invest in companies that have excellent track records with verifiable sales and earnings. Therefore most of them automatically cannot invest in IPOs. In the last several years however, mutual funds have been more "tolerant" towards the nature of the IPOs, that's because there are more and more investors who demand mutual funds that invest in IPOs. A lot of these mutual funds invest in private markets, providing early access to hot IPOs for retail investors. The downside is these investment products actually come with bigger risk, for worthy potential profit, of course.

Today, a lot of mutual funds already invest in IPOs, These are mutual funds that have aggressive growth profiles. However, usually only as a small part of a bigger portfolio of established growth stock companies. Aggressive growth means that these mutual funds will try to achieve the highest potential capital gains possible, that's why these mutual funds are also known as 'maximum capital gains funds' or 'capital appreciation funds'.

However, aiming for higher capital gains comes with a price, as they also come with bigger potential losses. Investments in these funds are companies that show potential high growth and usually come with a lot of share price mutability. But remember that these are only for those investors who are not reluctant to take a greater risk in order to expect higher capital gains in return.

Aggressive growth funds have a positive correlation with the stock market, during the economic upswings they tend to perform very well, while in economic downturns they could perform very poorly. When investing in a company's IPO they can quickly turn around and then re-sell the stock to gain great profits. There are also some aggressive growth funds that invest in options in order to boost returns.

These aggressive growth mutual funds have elevated the IPO investing trend in the recent years, especially with more and more popular names going public, like Alibaba, Twitter or Facebook. There are also other multibillion-dollar IPOs in the pipeline, including Airbnb, Uber and Palantir.

Investing in IPOs could be a huge source of high returns for investors, but it should be done with careful planning because these investments carry a great risk.

25. Can mutual funds outperform savings accounts?

Mutual funds can absolutely outperform a savings account. No matter how high the interest rate you get from your savings account, it's still not an investment. That means savings accounts won't even come close to mutual funds when it comes to making profits. However, savings accounts are definitely much safer compared to mutual funds. There's no chance for you to get rich just by having a savings account, but you don't have to worry about losing your money for bad investment decisions. Mutual fund investments come with a risk but they provide reliable returns that could make your money grows.

You need to understand exactly how they work if you want to decide whether it's best to choose a mutual fund or savings account for your financial needs. Everyone is probably already familiar with savings accounts, there are many different types of them at various banks. Usually by maintaining a high minimum balance you could get higher interest rates. While in mutual fund, the investment firm will gather your money with other investors' and then use the collective fund to invest in bonds, stocks or other securities. Each of these investors has a number of shares in the mutual fund that could be redeemed.

There is no risk when you put your money in a savings account, even when the bank collapsed you still can get your money back, because your fund is insured. On the other hand, stocks, bonds and other securities where your money will be invested through a mutual fund are quite unpredictable. However, as said before, you could get a good amount of profit compared to a savings account where you only expect a small profit from interest rates. If you don't want to take a higher risk but still want to make some nice profits, you could consider a money market fund, which is a type of mutual fund with lower risk. This type of mutual fund only invests in treasury notes and government securities.

So even a savings account that offers the highest rate that usually comes with a set of strict qualifications like withdrawal fees and minimum balance, still can't offer the same earning potentials like a mutual fund. Not to mention that you actually also have to pay for monthly maintenance fees for your savings account that will cut your low interest return. In mutual fund or any other type of investment product in that matter, risk and return always go hand in hand. Stocks and bonds are obviously offering much higher returns, although there are also some fees in a mutual fund, the returns are still much higher than what can be expected from a savings account.

Savings accounts are created and maintained at banking institutions, where they are insured by the FDIC (Federal Deposit Insurance Corporation). Therefore in case there's a financial crisis and the banks don't have the cash to back up their deposits, their depositors can still get their money. While mutual funds that are maintained in investment firms are not covered by the FDIC.

26. Can mutual funds invest in private companies?

Although perhaps a bit surprising for many investors, mutual funds do can invest in private companies. Most mutual funds only use a tiny portion of their assets to invest in private companies, however in 2015 more mutual funds are showing great interest in various private startups and the trend keeps going up.

A lot of large mutual fund companies are trying to set themselves apart from index funds by making big investments in private companies. A lot of these companies have made huge profits by investing in some of the most successful startups like Uber or Pinterest. However, not all of them could enjoy the same level of success, in fact many mutual funds have suffered great failure with this move.

As they try to stay ahead of the index funds, a lot of mutual funds are actually betting on the early growth of new startups. These are basically startups that they believe will be the next superstars. However, just like many other startups, these young companies often have to struggle in the early going and obviously they're not always successful leaving their investors with little or no profit. However, most analysts believe that the temptation of finding the next superstar startups is much stronger than the fear of the risks.

Investing in private companies during the early stage carries a lot of risks, but this is also the stage where most investment opportunities exist. Therefore it would be a smart move for an investor to put his money in these private companies through an angel investment group or investment group. This way the investor can minimize the risk because it will be spread across many firms.

The Internet is a great source for investors to find these private companies and all kinds of information relating to their business models and operations. There are many websites that provide a place for buyers and sellers of these private companies to meet, and they also provide a lot of information about these companies. Furthermore, you can also use the Internet to find other useful information about these startups. You can visit these companies' websites to get some basic information and you can also read some online articles, blogs or forum that discuss these companies.

Additionally you can also get some great information from small or private business brokers who specialize in startup investing. You obviously will be given a lot of information by your mutual fund manager regarding the private company where the investment will be made, but it's always best if you can gather your information from many different valid sources just to get a clear picture of you're getting into.

Investing in private companies offers a lot of opportunities for investors to thrive, however it also comes with a big risk, because basically you will be funding an idea with little or no proven track records, so it's either you find the next big think or the next big flop. Just make sure you know what you're running into before making any move.

27. Does index trading increase market vulnerability?

There is a high possibility that index trading will increase market vulnerability, because it will boost correlations between stocks. Nowadays more and more investors are applying passive investing tactics in ETF (Exchange Traded Funds) as well as mutual funds because they offer lower costs and a simpler trading system. The assets and stocks held in these funds are traded as baskets over the market, which finally boosts the convergence of the individual stocks' equity betas. Many observers consider that it will definitely increase the systematic risk in the market.

Mutual funds and ETFs that track indexes are using passive management, which is the opposite of active management that has a manager to set the course of the investment and actively trading the assets as a way to beat the returns of these indexes. Investment funds controlled with a passive management offering certain market exposure for investors. They will increase the investors' portfolio diversification easily and lower the management fees.

These funds are trading large baskets of assets and stocks during the day in order to track indexes. The correlations and equity betas of different stocks will increase due to this similar stocks' trading in large baskets. When the stocks move simultaneously towards the same direction, then we have increased correlation, which will also increase systematic risk.

There are some reasons why passive management is considered as the ideal investment management style in this case. Less risk and lower management costs are two of them. But it's also because usually these investors believe in the efficient market hypothesis. In this hypothesis, it's stated that markets reflect and incorporate all information at all times, making the individual stock picking pretty much pointless. Therefore, investing in index funds is considered as the best strategy for these investors. Even though there are some other opposing theories, historically this strategy has outperformed most actively managed funds.

As stated above, many observers and analysts believe that passive investment funds are increasing systematic risk, which is the type of risk that's difficult to predict. Systematic risk is an inherent risk to the entire market in an entire market segment. It's also known as market risk, volatility or un-diversifiable risk. Systematic risk affects not only a particular industry or particular stock, but the overall market. Not only very difficult to predict, but this type of risk is pretty much impossible to be avoided completely. You cannot lessen the impact of this risk simply by diversification, it can only be done through the right asset allocation strategy. Very much different with unsystematic risk that only affects a specific individual security or group of securities. The impact of unsystematic risk could be mitigated simply through diversification.

As of 2011, ETFs had about 1.5 trillion dollar under management. Because these funds are trading assets and stocks in large baskets, a market shock to certain index or a popular company could bleed easily to other assets that have high correlations. That's the reason why index trading could definitely increase market vulnerability.

28. What is the difference between passive and active asset management?

Passive asset management and active asset management are two main investment strategies used by investors to generate profits. While active asset management is focusing to outperform a benchmark like the S&P 500 Index for example, passive asset management is aiming to mimic the asset holdings of a certain benchmark index.

By implementing an active asset management strategy, investors and portfolio managers are buying and selling securities like stocks, futures and options in order to outperform benchmark indexes. This type of investment management strategy is involving market trends, political data and economic analysis as well as specific news about certain companies. The active management system has a manager who's responsible in generating greater returns from the investment compared to fund managers who mainly mimic the holdings of securities, such as stocks futures and futures that are listed on an index. It can also be considered as a high-cost investment, because the management fees on funds and active portfolios are quite high.

The investment manager in active asset management system is a crucial figure with a great responsibility to set the course of the investment strategy. The manager in active investment should always pay close attention to economic changes, market trends and even staying up to date with any development in political landscape or other factors that could affect certain companies and industries. This data could help in determining the best time to buy or sell the investments in order to make the highest profit as possible by taking advantage of irregularities. This type of investment strategy could be considered as an aggressive strategy, that's why it has a higher potential to bring bigger profit. However, this huge profit potential comes with a price, if not managed carefully, it may result in little or no profit for the investors. With high management fees, small profit is definitely not an option for the investors.

Passive asset management on the other hand, is quite the opposite of the active asset management. In this type of investment strategy, the fund manager will only purchase assets that are listed on a benchmark index. The approach of this investment strategy is to allocate a portfolio mimicking a market index as well as applying a similar weighting as the index. Rather than trying to outperform the benchmark index like in active asset management, passive asset management is just targeting to generate the same returns as the chosen index.

For example, if a passively managed fund is aiming to mimic the performance of the Russell 1000 index, the fund manager will manage the ETF by simply buying large cap stocks listed on the Russell 1000 index. The investments are not meant to outperform the Russell 1000, but just trying managed to generate similar returns as the Russell 1000. This kind of strategy has a low expense ratio because it's passively managed and also has a low turnover ratio. Both active and passive management strategies have their own advantages and disadvantages, which one is better than the other? It pretty much depends on each investor's point of view.

Ref9 Chapter Nine - Frequently Asked Questions (Mutual Funds) as researched and written by the author Ronald E. Hudkins www.RonaldHudkins.com

Appendix I

Glossary of Key Mutual Fund Terms

12b-1 Fees — fees paid by the fund out of fund assets to cover the costs of marketing and selling fund shares and sometimes to cover the costs of providing shareholder services. "Distribution fees" include fees to compensate brokers and others who sell fund shares and to pay for advertising, the printing and mailing of prospectuses to new investors, and the printing and mailing of sales literature. "Shareholder Service Fees" are fees paid to persons to respond to investor inquiries and provide investors with information about their investments.

Account Fee — a fee that some funds separately impose on investors for the maintenance of their accounts. For example, accounts below a specified dollar amount may have to pay an account fee.

Back-end Load — a sales charge (also known as a "deferred sales charge") investors pay when they redeem (or sell) mutual fund shares, generally used by the fund to compensate brokers.

Classes — different types of shares issued by a single fund, often referred to as Class A shares, Class B shares, and so on. Each class invests in the same "pool" (or investment portfolio) of securities and has the same investment objectives and policies. But each class has different shareholder services and/or distribution arrangements with different fees and expenses and therefore different performance results.

Closed-End Fund — a type of investment company that does not continuously offer its shares for sale but instead sells a fixed number of shares at one time (in the initial public offering) which then typically trade on a secondary market, such as the New York Stock Exchange or the Nasdaq Stock Market. Legally known as a "closed-end company."

Contingent Deferred Sales Load — a type of back-end load, the amount of which depends on the length of time the investor held his or her shares. For example, a contingent deferred sales load might be (X)% if an investor holds his or her shares for one year, (X-1)% after two years, and so on until the load reaches zero and goes away completely.

Conversion — a feature some funds offer that allows investors to automatically change from one class to another (typically with lower annual expenses) after a set period of time. The fund's prospectus or profile will state whether a class ever converts to another class.

Deferred Sales Charge — see "back-end load" (above).

Distribution Fees — fees paid out of fund assets to cover expenses for marketing and selling fund shares, including advertising costs, compensation for brokers and others who sell fund shares, and payments for printing and mailing prospectuses to new investors and sales literature prospective investors. Sometimes referred to as "12b-1 fees."

Exchange Fee — a fee that some funds impose on shareholders if they exchange (transfer) to another fund within the same fund group.

Exchange-Traded Funds — a type of an investment company (either an open-end company or UIT) whose objective is to achieve the same return as a particular market index. ETFs differ from traditional open-end companies and UITs, because, pursuant to SEC exemptive orders, shares issued by ETFs trade on a secondary market and are only redeemable from the fund itself in very large blocks (blocks of 50,000 shares for example).

Expense Ratio — the fund's total annual operating expenses (including management fees, distribution (12b-1) fees, and other expenses) expressed as a percentage of average net assets.

Front-end Load — an upfront sales charge investors pay when they purchase fund shares, generally used by the fund to compensate brokers. A front-end load reduces the amount available to purchase fund shares.

Index Fund — describes a type of mutual fund or Unit Investment Trust (UIT) whose investment objective typically is to achieve the same return as a particular market index, such as the S&P 500 Composite Stock Price Index, the Russell 2000 Index, or the Wilshire 5000 Total Market Index.

Investment Adviser — generally, a person or entity who receives compensation for giving individually tailored advice to a specific person on investing in stocks, bonds, or mutual funds. Some investment advisers also manage portfolios of securities, including mutual funds.

Investment Company — a company (corporation, business trust, partnership, or limited liability company) that issues securities and is primarily engaged in the business of investing in securities. The three basic types of investment companies are mutual funds, closed-end funds, and unit investment trusts.

Load — see "Sales Charge."

Management Fee — fee paid out of fund assets to the fund's investment adviser or its affiliates for managing the fund's portfolio, any other management fee payable to the fund's investment adviser or its affiliates, and any administrative fee payable to the investment adviser that are not included in the "Other Expenses" category. A fund's management fee appears as a category under "Annual Fund Operating Expenses" in the Fee Table.

Market Index — a measurement of the performance of a specific "basket" of stocks considered to represent a particular market or sector of the U.S. stock market or the economy. For example, the Dow Jones Industrial Average (DJIA) is an index of 30 "blue chip" U.S. stocks of industrial companies (excluding transportation and utility companies).

Mutual Fund — the common name for an open-end investment company. Like other types of investment companies, mutual funds pool money from many investors and invest the money in stocks, bonds, short-term money-market instruments, or other securities. Mutual funds issue redeemable shares that investors purchase directly from the fund (or through a broker for the fund) instead of purchasing from investors on a secondary market.

NAV (Net Asset Value) — the value of the fund's assets minus its liabilities. SEC rules require funds to calculate the NAV at least once daily. To calculate the NAV per share, simply subtract the fund's liabilities from its assets and then divide the result by the number of shares outstanding.

No-load Fund — a fund that does not charge any type of sales load. But not every type of shareholder fee is a "sales load," and a no-load fund may charge fees that are not sales loads. No-load funds also charge operating expenses.

Open-End Company — the legal name for a mutual fund. An open-end company is a type of investment company

Operating Expenses — the costs a fund incurs in connection with running the fund, including management fees, distribution (12b-1) fees, and other expenses.

Portfolio — an individual's or entity's combined holdings of stocks, bonds, or other securities and assets.

Profile — summarizes key information about a mutual fund's costs, investment objectives, risks, and performance. Although every mutual fund has a prospectus, not every mutual fund has a profile.

Prospectus — describes the mutual fund to prospective investors. Every mutual fund has a prospectus. The prospectus contains information about the mutual fund's costs, investment objectives, risks, and performance. You can get a prospectus from the mutual fund company (through its website or by phone or mail). Your financial professional or broker can also provide you with a copy.

Purchase Fee — a shareholder fee that some funds charge when investors purchase mutual fund shares. Not the same as (and may be in addition to) a front-end load.

Redemption Fee — a shareholder fee that some funds charge when investors redeem (or sell) mutual fund shares. Redemption fees (which must be paid to the fund) are not the same as (and may be in addition to) a back-end load (which is typically paid to a broker). The SEC generally limits redemption fees to 2%.

Sales Charge (or "Load") — the amount that investors pay when they purchase (front-end load) or redeem (back-end load) shares in a mutual fund, similar to a commission. The SEC's rules do not limit the size of sales load a fund may charge, but FINRA rules state that mutual fund sales loads cannot exceed 8.5% and must be even lower depending on other fees and charges assessed.

Shareholder Service Fees — fees paid to persons to respond to investor inquiries and provide investors with information about their investments. See also "12b-1 fees."

Statement of Additional Information (SAI) — conveys information about an open- or closed-end fund that is not necessarily needed by investors to make an informed investment decision, but that some investors find useful. Although funds are not required to provide investors with the SAI, they must give investors the SAI upon request and without charge. Also known as "Part B" of the fund's registration statement.

Total Annual Fund Operating Expense — the total of a fund's annual fund operating expenses, expressed as a percentage of the fund's average net assets. You'll find the total in the fund's fee table in the prospectus.

Unit Investment Trust (UIT) — a type of investment company that typically makes a one-time "public offering" of only a specific, fixed number of units. A UIT will terminate and dissolve on a date established when the UIT is created (although some may terminate more than fifty years after they are created). UITs do not actively trade their investment portfolios.

10 BEST RESOURCES ON THE WEB: DIVERSIFY YOUR PORTFOLIO TO MANAGE RISK AND MAXIMIZE RETURN

WASHINGTON, D.C.//September 25, 2013//Want to learn more about how to diversify your portfolio and how often to do it? A good place to turn for help is "A Diversified Portfolio – What You Need to Know and Investing Options" from the nonprofit Alliance for Investor Education (AIE) at http://www.investoreducation.org/diversification.

AIE is a consortium of 20 leading U.S. financial-related foundations, nonprofit organizations, associations and governmental agencies.

AIE President Don Blandin, who also serves as president of the Investor Protection Trust (IPT) and the Investor Protection Institute (IPI), said: "Diversification is widely recognized as key to minimizing risk and maximizing returns. The Alliance for Investor Education wants to make sure that all Americans have the best available information on how to diversify both their overall assets and how to diversify within their investment portfolio. Whether you are investing on your own or working with a qualified professional, this resource is a valuable tool to use as you start investing or review your existing asset allocation."

The new "A Diversified Portfolio – What You Need to Know and Investing Options" section of the AIE Web site features the following 10 top resources for consumers:

Building Your Portfolio: Using Diversification - Financial Industry Regulatory Authority. When you diversify, you divide the money you've allocated to a particular asset class, such as stocks, among various categories of investments that belong to that asset class. These smaller groups are called subclasses. Diversification, with its emphasis on variety, allows you to manage nonsystematic risk by tapping into the potential strength of different subclasses, which, like the larger asset classes, tend to do better in some periods than in others.

Portfolio Rebalancing: Diversification, Risk Control and Withdrawals - American Association of Individual Investors. Rebalancing reduces a portfolio's risk by maintaining the benefits of diversification, taking advantage of lower valuations and providing an alternative to panic in the midst of a bear market.

Handling Market Volatility - 360 Degrees of Financial Literacy/ American Institute of Certified Public Accountants. Diversifying your investment portfolio is one of the key ways you can handle market volatility.

Should You Be Using ETFs? - CFA Institute. Many investors have found that exchange-traded funds, or ETFs, are one of the more straightforward ways to add broad diversification to their portfolios.

5 Keys to Investing Success - Investor Protection Trust. Key #5 is diversify. Simply put, diversifying means not putting all your investment eggs in one basket. By spreading your investments around, you're likely to increase your overall return and reduce your risk at the same time.

Are Your Savings Investments Over-weighted? - American Savings Education Council/Employee Benefit Research Institute. Different types of investments—different funds—grow at different rates over time. Over time, those differences can add up—

leaving your retirement account weighted differently than you intended between stocks and bonds.

Savings & Investments - National Endowment for Financial Education. Managing risks and diversifying your assets is important even in retirement. NEFE provides tips on assessing your personal situation.

Futures Market Basics - U.S. Commodity Futures Trading Commission. If you decide to explore futures as part of a diversification strategy, the CFTC encourages you to make this decision great care and study.

Mutual Funds: A Guide for Investors - U.S. Securities and Exchange Commission. Mutual funds can offer the advantages of diversification and professional management. This brochure explains the basics of mutual fund investing - how mutual funds work, what factors to consider before investing, and how to avoid common pitfalls.

Opportunity and Risk: A Educational Guide to Trading Futures and Options on Futures - National Futures Association. This guide describes how futures and options on futures contracts are traded and the various ways investors can participate in the futures markets.

For an overview of the rest of the best investor education resources on the Web from AIE members, go to http://www.investoreducation.org.

ABOUT AIE

Founded in 1996, the Alliance for Investor Education Web site at http://www.investoreducation.org provides investors with access to a full range of information they need to make wise investment decisions. The 22-member Alliance for Investor Education is dedicated to facilitating greater understanding of investing, investments and the financial markets among current and prospective investors of all ages. We pursue initiatives for education and join with others to motivate Americans to obtain objective information and increase their knowledge and understanding of investing.

Full members of the Alliance include: American Association of Individual Investors, American Institute of Certified Public Accountants/360 Degrees of Financial Literacy, American Savings Education

Council/ Employee Benefit Research Institute, CFA Institute, Certified Financial Planner Board of Standards, Inc., Financial Industry Regulatory Authority, Investment Company Institute Education Foundation, Investor Protection Trust/Investor Protection Institute, National Association of Real Estate Investment Trusts, National Endowment for Financial Education, National Futures Association, Options Industry Council, SIFMA Foundation, Securities Investor Protection Corporation, and the Society for Financial Education and Professional Development.

The U.S. Securities and Exchange Commission, U.S. Commodity Futures Trading Commission, the U.S. Federal Trade Commission's Bureau of Consumer Protection, the Board of Governors of the Federal Reserve System, and the North American Securities Administrators Association are the governmental and quasi-governmental advisors to the Alliance.

CONTACT: Ailis Aaron Wolf, for AIE, (703) 276-3265 or aawolf@hastingsgroup.com.

Appendix III

There's An App for That

With today's World of smartphones and tablets being so useful in managing personal matters, David Bergmann, CFP® thought he would take the opportunity to share with you some business and personal 'Apps' for those smartphones and tablets that he thinks are really cool.

Bloomberg Mobile. This business news app is free, and users go to it for real-time financial market data, company descriptions and the latest market news and stock quotes. Advisors can use the "my stocks" feature to create personalized portfolios of stocks to follow for themselves or clients

1. Nest Egg Estimator. This is one of Android's top 10 apps. It's a great retirement tool because it projects finances into future years showing income, taxes, assets and debt. It also allows you to try different scenarios such as purchases, expenses, job changes and more.

2. Flipboard Pages. This iPad app delivers content from a number of

publications, including ABC News, All Things Digital, Bon Appétit, Lonely Planet, SB Nation, SF Gate, Uncrate and The Washington Post Magazine. When an article from one of those publishers is shared on Twitter or Facebook, a Flipboard user selects "Read Article," and can thus stay up to date on the latest news and magazine content in the financial industry.

3. Hootsuite. "Hootsuite is king when it comes to social media convenience and efficiency. Instead of shifting back and forth between social media platforms, Hootsuite allows admins to oversee and access all of their social operations in one convenient place.

4. Mint Mobile Apps. Easy organization of your finances—automatic categorization of your transactions—plus active, zoom able charts and graphs.

5. Droid PDF Scan. A document scanner wherever you are.

6. CamCard can capture business card images with a phone-based camera,

recognize the card image content, and automatically save the contact info in the phone's address book and Card Holder. In addition, CamCard contains many useful features, such as email signature recognition and QR code generation and recognition.

7. Visual Records has made it quick and simple to track and manage your vehicle mileage for tax/business purposes. This app can track and manage Vehicle Types, Trip Types and Mileage information; duplicate previous mileage records; add specific notes for each record; and export mileage information, which can be saved and sent via e-mail.

8. Pixetell allows you to quickly add voice, screen recordings and video to e-mail or documents, giving you the opportunity to go beyond written text when explaining forms, proposals and designs verbally. Pixetell allows you to combine voice, screen recordings and webcam delivered through a URL in your e-mail.

9. Mavenlink is an online collaboration solution that allows you to manage projects from start to finish, including communications, docs, tasks, scheduling, time tracking, invoicing and payments. Mavenlink integrates with Google Docs, Calendar, and Contacts. Your networks, communications, project notifications, due dates, and deliverables related to your working world are captured in one place: your Mavenlink dashboard.

10. Vlingo. Tell your phone what to do! The Vlingo Virtual Assistant turns your words into action. Vlingo combines voice to text technology with its "intent engine" to help you quickly complete your desired action. Simply speak to your phone or type a command through the ActionBar to get just about anything done while on the go.

11. Barcode Scanner. Scan barcodes on products then look up prices and reviews. You can also scan Data Matrix and QR Codes containing URLs, contact info, etc.

12. Lookout Mobile Security helps you protect your phone and includes Anti-Virus, Backup and Find My Phone. The app allows you to block viruses, malware and spyware by scanning every app you download. Backup allows you to back up your contacts and photos, as well as restore data to a new or existing phone. Find My Phone can help you pinpoint your phone on a map, activate a loud alarm to find your phone, and if necessary remotely wipe your data if your phone is lost or stolen.

13. Seek Droid allows you to locate your lost or stolen device anywhere in the world. See your device on a map, set off an audible alarm, wipe the device, and more.

14. Wallet allows you to safely store all your sensitive data such as bank account details and passwords on your phone. Wallet is also useful for remembering all those bits and pieces of information in one place from

frequent flier numbers to contact lens prescriptions.

15.   Spotlight Six Software makes it easy to track your billable hours as you are working and then transfer the data into a spreadsheet to create your invoices. This app calculates hours worked and wages. Users can create customizable reports that can be exported via e-mail and view and edit time records within the app, among other things.

16.   Long Term Care. The Genworth Cost of Care App provides a convenient way to view long-term care cost details in today's dollars across various care settings, compare costs across multiple locations and estimate future long-term care costs. The App allows users to: (1) View long-term care costs on a daily, monthly and annual basis for 437 regions across the United States (2) View care costs in different care settings, including in-home care, Adult Day Health Care, Assisted Living Facility, and Nursing Home Care (3) Estimate future costs up to

30 years out (4) Compare care costs across multiple locations and (6) Use geo-locate functionality to automatically locate an area within the U.S.

17.   Mortgage Calculator. Choose four calculators (1) rent or buy, (2) debt to income calculator, (3) monthly payment calculator, (4) refinance calculator and (5) the ability to search for homes.

18.   Morningstar. The content for this application is provided by Morningstar.com – helping investors reach their financial goals – with comprehensive investment research and tools covering U.S. and Canadian stocks, mutual funds, ETFs, options, hedge funds, commodities and portfolio management.

19.   Kiplinger. For more than 50 years, Kiplinger has been giving readers practical advice on investing, saving, budgeting, credit, spending and more. Now you can enjoy the same money-smart advantage with

this convenient interactive app for your iPad.

Extracted from
http://www.plannersearch.org/life-events/financial-planning/There's%20An%20App%20for%20That courtesy of the Financial Planning Association > Life Events > CatalogItem-796695515

Appendix IV

Beginners' Guides to Investing: Online Publications at the SEC

Get the Facts: The SEC's Roadmap to Saving and Investing. This is your roadmap to starting on a journey of financial security through saving and investing.
http://www.sec.gov/investor/pubs/roadmap.htm

Ask Questions: Questions You Should Ask About Your Investments and What To Do If You Run Into Problems. Questions you should ask about investment products and the people who sell those products with tips on how to monitor your investments.
http://www.sec.gov/investor/pubs/askquestions.htm
http://www.sec.gov/pdf/pregunte.pdf ("Ask Questions" brochure in Spanish)

Taking Stock: Getting Your Fiscal Act Together. For Investors, this is a good time to take stock of where you are and where you want to be, and plan how best to get there.
http://www.sec.gov/investor/pubs/takingstock.htm

The SEC Mutual Fund Cost Calculator: A Tool for Comparing Mutual Funds. The Mutual Fund Cost Calculator enables investors to easily estimate and compare costs of owning mutual funds.
http://www.sec.gov/investor/tools/mfcc/mfcc-int.htm

View More Information on Different Types of Investments:
http://www.sec.gov/investor/pubs/investop.htm

View More Investor Education Publications:
http://www.sec.gov/investor/pubs_subject.shtml

Check Out Your Broker or Adviser

Invest Wisely: Advice From Your Securities Industry Regulators. Before making a securities investment, you must decide which brokerage firm and sales representative-also referred to as a stockbroker, account executive, or registered representative-to use.
http://www.sec.gov/investor/pubs/inws.htm

Protect Your Money: Check Out Brokers and Advisers. Before you invest, make sure

your brokers, investment advisers, and investment advisers' representatives are licensed to sell securities.
http://www.sec.gov/investor/brokers.htm

View More Materials on Brokers
http://www.sec.gov/investor/pubs_subject.shtml/#brokers

View More Materials on Advisers
http://www.sec.gov/investor/pubs_subject.shtml#invad

Research Your Company's Stock

Beginners' Guide to Financial Statements. This brochure will help you gain a basic understanding of how to read financial statements.
http://www.sec.gov/investor/pubs/begfinstmtguide.htm

Getting Info About Companies. Learn how to get information about companies from a variety of sources; this publication covers corporate reports, reference books, and commercial databases that provide information.
http://www.sec.gov/investor/pubs/companies.htm

How Do I Use EDGAR? This is a tutorial to guide you through searching the SEC's online database of company reports.
http://www.sec.gov/edgar/quickedgar.htm

Information Matters. This publication describes the information you should review before you invest, provides tips on how to find information about companies and lists several "red flags" to avoid.
http://www.sec.gov/answers/infomatters.htm

Information About Some Companies Not Available From the SEC. The federal securities laws require most publicly traded companies to register their securities and file reports with the SEC. This document describes how investors can find information on privately held companies and companies that are exempt from the SEC's registration requirements.
http://www.sec.gov/answers/noinfo.htm

View More Investor Education Materials
http://www.sec.gov/investor/pubs_subject.shtml

Help and How to File a Complaint at the SEC

SEC Center for Complaints and Enforcement Tips. Report suspicious activity, file a complaint about a financial professional or an investment product, or ask questions. The division of Enforcement and The Office of Investor Education and Advocacy created the SEC complaint center to address your concerns.
http://www.sec.gov/complaint.shtml

The SEC's Office of Investor Education and Advocacy. Our office acts as your gateway to the SEC. We cannot tell you what investments to make, but we can tell you how to invest wisely and protect your hard earned investment dollars from securities fraud and abuse. If you have suffered wrongdoing at the hands of a bad broker or investment adviser, we want to hear from you.
http://www.sec.gov/investor/pubs/aboutoiea.htm

The Investor's Advocate: How the SEC Protects Investors and Maintains Market Integrity. The laws and rules that govern the securities industry in the United States derive from a simple and straightforward concept: all investors, whether large institutions or private individuals, should have access to certain basic facts about an investment prior to buying it. http://www.sec.gov/about/whatwedo.shtml

Extracted November 9, 2015 from the Internet @ http://www.sec.gov/investor/pubs/begininvest.htm

Acknowledgements

I would like to personally thank the agencies and authors that provided their research, expertise, financial proficiency and expert advice that made the compilation of this book possible.

Wikipedia, the free encyclopedia @ "https://en.wikipedia.org/w/index.php?title=Mutual_fund&oldid=693572545

The U.S. Securities and Exchange Commission, @ http://www.sec.gov/investor/pubs/

Financial Planning Association > Life Events > Catalog Item-796695515 @ http://www.plannersearch.org/life-events/financial-planning/investments/Don't%20Put%20All%20Your%20Apples%20in%20One%20Basket article written by Ara Oghoorian, CFA, CFP®

Common Investment Abuses By FPA member Tim Sobolewski, CFP®, The Financial Planning Center, Amherst, NY and Joanne Schultz, Esq., of Williamsville NY. @

http://www.plannersearch.org/life-events/financial-planning/investments/Common%20Investment%20Abuses

Thank you most sincerely,

Ronald E. Hudkins

About the Author

Ronald E. Hudkins (1951-Present) now residing in Durango, Colorado was born in Canton, Ohio and raised in Massillon, Ohio. He was drafted into military service in 1970 where he remained up until 1993 when he retired honorably from the U.S. Army, Military Police Corps. During his service, after and in between a lot of traveling he attended many universities that include Kent State

University, Maryland University, Central Texas College (European Branch), Blair Junior College, Hagerstown Junior College and Phoenix University. He

*The Author
Ronald E. Hudkins*

declared two majors in the areas of Business Administration and a Bachelor of Science in Information Technology.

Ronald has been writing as a hobby for over twenty years. He has completed a collection of multiple genres in both fiction and nonfiction that include financial, estate, cooking and identity theft. In the area of fiction he has published humor, science fiction and fantasy. He is polishing up some children's, paranormal romance, romance and additional science fiction books. He has approximately 50 additional plot outlines completed and their associated books in various stages of completion. We can anticipate more stories in the areas of finance, children's and young adult reading as well as humor, fantasy, romance, thrillers and even some mystery and steampunk. Only the author's files and mind know the definitive creations yet to be.

He is a Platinum Level Expert author at http://ezinearticles.com/expert=Ronald_Hudkins where he has published over 100 articles in 29 separate niches which have amassed over 74,000 views.

He participates on social sites, such as Facebook and Twitter, videos on YouTube and slid presentations too many and numerous to list. Needless to say, he stays occupied and busy and as such - we all benefit. See his other projects page on his

Author's Other Books

Listed at (Amazon Books)
http://www.amazon.com/-/e/B00J158MSM

(Barnes & Noble)
http://www.barnesandnoble.com/s/%22Ron
ald%20E%20Hudkins%22?Ns=P_Sales_Rank
&Ntk=P_key_Contributor_List&Ntx=mode%2
0matchall

(Author website)
http://www.ronaldhudkins.com/index.html

(Fiction Categories)

Children's Books

Two Different Pictures (Activity Book),
Book 16, Published August 28, 2014

The World Outside (Adventure), Book 17,
Published September 16, 2014

Fantasy

The Cape Coral Heroes, Book 9, Published March 19, 2014

Humor

Senior Things I Said, Say, Did and Do, Book 3 published December 21, 2013

The Summer of Lost Soles, Book 4, published March 20, 2013

Science Fiction

The Thirty Century War, Book 5, published November 16, 2013

Paranormal Romance (Teen)

The River of Love – Surfacing, Book 7, Published (April 11, 2015)

Coloring Books for Grown-Ups

The Grown-Ups Coloring Book - **Geometric Designs Volume # 1**

The Grown-Ups Coloring Book - **Geometric Designs Volume # 2**

The Grown-Ups Coloring Book - **Geometric Designs Volume # 1**

The Grown-Ups Coloring Book – **Alice in Wonderland Book # 4**

The Grown-Ups Coloring Book – **The Looking Glass Book # 5**

The Grown-Ups Coloring Book – **Floral Patterns Book #6**

Romance (Erotica Adult)

Stay the Night, Book 10, Published May 10, 2014

Longing Love and Coming Home, Book 15, Published August 24, 2014

Steampunk

The First Steampunk Adventures – Tales One thru Five, Book 22, Published May 21, 2015

The Second Steampunk Adventures – Tales Six thru 10, Book 23, projected February 2016

Thriller, Murder, Suspense

<u>The Sapiens Missile Murder Mystery</u>,
Book 30, published November 18, 2015

(Nonfiction Categories)

Computer References

<u>Your Digital Footprint – Password</u>
<u>Protection Requirements</u>, Book 11,
Published June 12, 2014

Cookbooks

<u>What Makes Cannabis Recipes Work</u>,
Book 6, Published December 26, 2013

<u>100 Easy Holiday Platters for New</u>
<u>Year's</u>, Book 18, Published January 20,
2015

Financial References (Teen and Young Adult)

<u>Basic Savings and Checking Account</u>
<u>Maintenance</u> – Book One for Teens and

Young Adults, Book 8, Published March 7, 2014

Basic Budget Establishment and Maintenance – Book Two for Teens and Young Adults, Book 19, Published February Four, 2015

Understanding Penny Stock Market – Book Three for Teens and Young Adults, Book 12, Published August 22, 2014

Basic Understanding of the Stock Market – Book Four for Teens and Young Adults, Book 20, Published February 8, 2015

Basic Understanding of Bond Investments – Book Five for Teens and Young Adults, Book 21, Published February 22, 2015

Basic Understanding of Financial Investment – Book Six for Teens and Young Adults, Book 24, Published June 22, 2015

Basic Understanding of Mutual Funds – Book Seven for Teens and Young Adults, Pending January xx, 2016

Basic Understanding of Certificates of Deposit – Book Eight for Teens and Young Adults, Pending March xx, 2016

Self Help

Asset Protection and Estate Planning for All Ages, Book 1, Published July 12, 2007

How to Avoid Identity Theft, Book 2, Published June 15, 2011

Medical References

Lower Your High Blood Pressure Naturally Without a Prescription, Book 14, Published October 27, 2014

Pet References

45 Foods that Kill Your Dog and 21 Other Things, Book 13, Published August 12, 2014

Thank You for your Visit. Please refer your friends!!!

References

1.Chapter One – Mutual Funds Overview courtesy of Article titled - Invest Wisely: An Introduction to Mutual Funds posted by the U.S. Securities and Exchange Commission, November 2015 @ http://www.sec.gov/investor/pubs/inwsmf.htm

2.Chapter Two - courtesy of Article titled - Calculating Mutual Fund Fees and Expenses posted by the U.S. Securities and Exchange Commission, November 2015 @ http://www.sec.gov/investor/tools/mfcc/mfcc-int.htm

3.Chapter Three - courtesy of Article titled - Breakpoint Discounts posted by the U.S. Securities and Exchange Commission, November 2015 @ http://www.sec.gov/answers/breakpt.htm

4.Chapter Four - Avoiding Common Pitfalls courtesy of Publication titled – Mutual Funds, A Guide for Investors posted by the U.S. Securities and Exchange Commission, November 2015 @ https://www.sec.gov/investor/pubs/sec-guide-to-mutual-funds.pdf

5.Chapter Five - Transferring Your Brokerage Account: Tips on Avoiding Delays Investors posted by the U.S. Securities and Exchange Commission, November 2015 @ http://www.sec.gov/investor/pubs/acctxfer.htm

6. Chapter Six - Questions You Should Ask about Your Investments and What to Do If You Run into Problems posted by the U.S. Securities and Exchange Commission, November 2015 @ http://www.sec.gov/investor/pubs/askquestions.htm

7. Chapter Seven – Financial Planning Association > Life Events > Catalog Item- 796695515 @ http://www.plannersearch.org/life-events/financial-planning/investments/Don't%20Put%20All%20Your%20Apples%20in%20One%20Basket article written by Ara Oghoorian, CFA, CFP®

8. Chapter Eight - Common Investment Abuses By FPA member Tim Sobolewski, CFP®, The Financial Planning Center, Amherst, NY and Joanne Schultz, Esq., of Williamsville NY. Extracted from the Internet November 9, 2015 @

http://www.plannersearch.org/life-events/financial-planning/investments/Common%20Investment%20Abuses

9. Chapter Nine - Frequently Asked Questions (Mutual Funds) as researched and written by the author Ronald E. Hudkins www.RonaldHudkins.com

Book Review

Thank you for reading my book Basic Understanding of Mutual Funds Book Seven - for Teens and Young Adults. Please, if you liked the book take a spare moment as it would be a great help if you could post a review of it on Amazon @ (http://www.amazon.com/-/e/B00J158MSM) and let other potential readers know why you liked it. It's not necessary to write a lengthy, formal review—a summary of the comments from you would be perfectly fine.

Thank You